TURNING DEFEAT INTO VICTORY

Turning Defeat into Victory

M. MARTYRIA MADAUSS

KANAAN PUBLICATIONS
Evangelical Sisterhood of Mary
Darmstadt, Germany and Radlett, England

Original title: *Grund meiner Freude: Nachfolge im Licht des Römerbriefes Kap. 1-8; 12*
First German edition 1975

First British edition 1995
published by Kanaan Publications

ISBN 1 897647 09 3

Unless otherwise stated, all Bible quotations are taken from the Revised Standard Version of the Bible, copyrighted 1946 and 1952, and used by permission.

Bible quotations identified RAV are taken from the Holy Bible: Revised Authorised Version, The New King James Version. Copyright © 1979, 1980, 1982, Thomas Nelson, Inc., Publishers, and used by permission.

Designed and Produced in England by
Nuprint Ltd, Station Road, Harpenden, Herts AL5 4SE

CONTENTS

Introduction

Paul's Letter to the Romans was written to a church he did not yet know personally. The church in Rome was established neither by Paul nor by Peter, but most likely by Jews present in Jerusalem at Pentecost (Acts 2:10) and by travellers who had heard the Good News in other places and had brought it back to Rome (for example, Aquila and Priscilla, Acts 18:2). Paul had long wished to visit the Christian community in Rome, but had no opportunity to do so (Romans 1:13, 15; 15:22). Only later, as a prisoner, was he able to see the brothers there. They lovingly came out from the city to meet him, their affection no doubt partly inspired by this letter (Acts 28:15).

The Letter to the Romans was addressed to Gentile as well as Jewish Christians. It was delivered by Phoebe, a deaconess of the church at Cenchreae (16:1), and dictated to Tertius in Corinth at the end of Paul's third missionary journey (16:22).

Not only then but throughout the subsequent centuries the Letter to the Romans has helped to spread the foundations of the Christian faith. In his 'Preface to the Epistle of St. Paul to the Romans',

Martin Luther declares: 'This epistle is in truth the most important document in the New Testament, the gospel in its purest expression. Not only is it well worth a Christian's while to know it word for word by heart, but also to meditate on it day by day. It is the soul's daily bread . . . It may therefore be said that this epistle gives the richest possible account of what a Christian ought to know, namely, the meaning of law, gospel, sin, punishment, grace, faith, righteousness . . . It tells what our attitude should be to our fellows . . . and to our own selves . . . Therefore, every Christian ought to study Romans regularly and continuously. May God grant His grace to this end. Amen.'*

---

*Bertram Lee Woolf in *Reformation Writings of Martin Luther, Translated with Introduction and Notes from the Definitive Weimar Edition*, Vol. II, 'The Spirit of the Protestant Reformation', Philosophical Library, New York, pages 284, 299-300.

ROMANS
—— ONE ——

1:1-7

Paul, a servant of Jesus Christ, called to be an apostle, set apart for the gospel of God which he promised beforehand through his prophets in the holy scriptures, the gospel concerning his Son, who was descended from David according to the flesh and designated Son of God in power according to the Spirit of holiness by his resurrection from the dead, Jesus Christ our Lord, through whom we have received grace and apostleship to bring about the obedience of faith for the sake of his name among all the nations, including yourselves who are called to belong to Jesus Christ; To all God's beloved in Rome, who are called to be saints: Grace to you and peace from God our Father and the Lord Jesus Christ.

The apostle Paul describes himself, the author of the letter, as a bond-servant, a slave of Jesus Christ. He means that what he writes — no less than what the other apostles write — is the gospel of Jesus Christ. To stress his authority, Paul opens his letter by stating his calling as an apostle, for the letters of the apostles are regarded as the Word of God (1 Thessalonians 2:13).

What is Paul's mission as an apostle? — To

preach the gospel proclaimed by the prophets long ago: Grace has accomplished what God promised. The head of the serpent has been crushed by Jesus Christ (Genesis 3:15).

The glory of Jesus Christ was made manifest in this: Though descended from David physically, He was powerfully demonstrated to be the Son of God spiritually. In other words, despite the fact that He assumed human nature, there was no sin in Him, as the Spirit of God within Him verified in a striking manner when He rose from the dead. Death could not hold Him.

The same Spirit of God enkindles us with faith in Jesus Christ; and when the Holy Spirit brings this about, we experience resurrection life. Only then do we become able to obey God through faith and to do what He requires of us. Because we cannot obey God in our own strength, the apostle Paul wishes the Christians in Rome grace and peace from God our Father and the Lord Jesus Christ.

1:8-15
First, I thank my God through Jesus Christ for all of you, because your faith is proclaimed in all the world. For God is my witness, whom I serve with my spirit in the gospel of his Son, that without ceasing I mention you always in my prayers, asking that somehow by God's will I may now at last succeed in coming to you. For I long to see you, that I may impart to you some spiritual gift to strengthen you, that is, that we may be mutually encouraged by each other's faith, both yours and mine. I want

you to know, brethren, that I have often intended to come to you (but thus far have been prevented), in order that I may reap some harvest among you as well as among the rest of the Gentiles. I am under obligation both to Greeks and to barbarians, both to the wise and to the foolish: so I am eager to preach the gospel to you also who are in Rome.

Paul writes to the Christians in Rome in a spirit of love, prayer and gratitude. He opens his heart to them, identifying with them in brotherly affection as one who is completely in Jesus Christ. He desires to work among them and see some result of his labours. God does call people to preach the gospel so that others will believe and obey Him. So the apostle longs to fulfil his commission whenever and wherever the opportunity arises. It is the Holy Spirit compelling Paul. Thus he is prepared to come to Rome.

1:16-17

For I am not ashamed of the gospel: it is the power of God for salvation to every one who has faith, to the Jew first and also to the Greek. For in it the righteousness of God is revealed through faith for faith; as it is written, 'He who through faith is righteous shall live.'

Here the theme of the letter rings out. Although persecution has come upon the church in Rome, the apostle is not ashamed or afraid to proclaim the gospel. The good news of Christ is a mighty power which Paul has himself experienced and can testify to. The message of the cross (1 Corinthians 1:18) is dynamic. It saves, renews, transforms and brings joy. For a disciple of Jesus this means: The power of God will be revealed in me to the extent I accept the gospel of Christ, grasping the significance of Jesus' death on the cross in atonement for my sins. God's nature is love, both holy and merciful. It was this love of God that caused Him to sacrifice on our behalf His only begotten Son, Jesus Christ, so that through Him we might receive new life by faith. 'The righteous shall live by his faith' (Habakkuk 2:4). This means that we will find divine life by trusting God. Then we are in tune with God. Then we are not ashamed of the gospel, the good news that God pardons sinners. This is the source of our life and joy. All human sadness is a sign that we are not really in tune with God — that is, we are not willing to be pardoned sinners.

Paul spells out for us that only pardoned sinners are offered the righteousness of God. Incredibly, God makes us right in His sight when we put our trust in Christ to save us. God wants to impart His righteousness to us, as we can see from Jesus' words: 'You shall be perfect, just as your Father in heaven is perfect' (Matthew 5:48 RAV). Since God's righteousness is freely offered to us, we have nothing else to do but to accept it and lay hold of it by faith.

We receive the blessing of justification by faith when we long for God to make Himself known to us, when we hunger and thirst for His righteousness, because true faith always begins at the point where we reach out to receive Jesus Christ. Only the Spirit of God can awaken such faith in us — though we, for our part, must be willing and receptive, and then cling to Jesus Christ in faith.

It is God who inspires us with faith in the first place. But it is up to us to cling to Christ in faith and expect everything from Him alone, knowing how spiritually bankrupt we are and that we can do nothing in our own strength. Unbelief always stems from pride: We think we are strong. Faith can only take over when we see nothing good in ourselves and no change in our characters in spite of all our efforts and good intentions. Faith then makes us look to Jesus and His saving work, relying on Him alone. Faith is always active, drawing Jesus Christ into our lives as a reality — the One who delivered us from the power of Satan. The person who has faith is sorry about his sin, realizing that it hurts Jesus. At the same time he holds on to God's promise of forgiveness and to Jesus' act of redemption. He places all his confidence in Jesus Christ, the Friend of sinners. He realizes how immeasurably Jesus suffered to atone for our sins, and he gratefully accepts the salvation offered to him.

1:18
For the wrath of God is revealed from heaven against all
ungodliness and wickedness of men who by their
wickedness suppress the truth.

God's wrath is upon those who are not put right
with Him through faith — a fact that should spur
us on to trust in Him. The person who has faith is
saved from the wrath of God, because Jesus sub-
mitted Himself to the divine wrath, suffering it on
our behalf as the Lamb of God. Consequently, the
believer can be certain that no one can snatch him
from Jesus' hand, as long as he firmly remains
there in faith.

When is God's wrath upon us? When we push
the truth away from us (1:18) — that is, when we
resist the One who said of Himself, 'I am . . . the
truth' (John 14:6). Don't we know that uncomfort-
able feeling when Jesus meets us and shows us all
our sins, just as He did for the woman of Samaria
at Jacob's Well (John 4)? If we have a genuine
encounter with Jesus, He will reveal our sins to us.
But usually we try to avoid that searching glance of
His, which met Peter after he denied his Lord. We
don't want to be unmasked. Yet this is where the
struggle against sin should begin. With all our
hearts we should desire His light, no matter how
much it hurts. When Jesus gives us light, we draw
very close to Him, the Friend of sinners. The living
Jesus is always present when He reveals the whole

of our sinful nature to us. Only at such times do we have a real encounter with Him.

1:19-21

For what can be known about God is plain to them, because God has shown it to them. Ever since the creation of the world his invisible nature, namely, his eternal power and deity, has been clearly perceived in the things that have been made. So they are without excuse; for although they knew God they did not honour him as God or give thanks to him, but they became futile in their thinking and their senseless minds were darkened.

We stand exposed in our sinfulness when we fail to acknowledge God as Creator, when we fail to give Him the glory and honour that are His due. Then the wrath of God descends upon us.

In keeping with His love and holiness, God would have us honour Him. He grieves today, because mankind is robbing Him of His honour, glorifying mortal man and his achievements instead. This suffering which God endures should inspire us to do all we can to bring Him glory and praise. God desires our love. Through love we can avert His wrath — that is, by living for Him in loving devotion and holy fear. But if we are self-centred and lead a life detached from Him, everything we do is futile. Then we become slaves of the things absorbing our ego, and our minds are darkened. We call evil good and open the door to fear of the future.

1:22-23
Claiming to be wise, they became fools, and exchanged the glory of the immortal God for images resembling mortal man or birds or animals or reptiles.

Instead of worship being given to God, created things are worshipped and idolized. If we disregard God and cease to be dependent upon Him, He lets us go our own way and we become fools. What is more, without noticing it, many become not only idol-worshippers but blasphemers, even Satan-worshippers, as we are seeing today. It's an either-or situation.

1:24-32
Therefore God gave them up in the lusts of their hearts to impurity, to the dishonouring of their bodies among themselves, because they exchanged the truth about God for a lie and worshipped and served the creature rather than the Creator, who is blessed for ever! Amen.

For this reason God gave them up to dishonourable passions. Their women exchanged natural relations for unnatural, and the men likewise gave up natural relations with women and were consumed with passion for one another, men committing shameless acts with men and receiving in their own persons the due penalty for their error.

And since they did not see fit to acknowledge God, God gave them up to a base mind and to improper conduct. They were filled with all manner of wickedness, evil, covetousness, malice. Full of envy, murder, strife, deceit, malignity, they are gossips, slanderers, haters of God, insolent, haughty, boastful, inventors of evil, disobedient to parents, foolish, faithless, heartless, ruthless. Though they know God's decree that those who do such things deserve to die, they not only do them but approve those who practise them.

You cannot make a fool of God. When He is no longer the focal point, everything collapses. When reverence for God departs, a whole nation incurs His wrath: He abandons that nation. He allows sin to run its course as an act of judgment. When created things are idolized, man ends up debasing, defiling and destroying himself. When God is rejected, man's evil mind is dominant. At variance with itself, it is capable only of tormenting others. A clearer demonstration of this than the present state of mankind is hard to imagine.

Abandonment to sin leads to death and hell. Either we are completely dedicated to Jesus, or Satan makes good his claim on us. Either we are justified by faith and have peace with God through our Lord Jesus Christ, or the wrath of God is upon us.

ROMANS
——TWO——

2:1-5
*Therefore you have no excuse, O man, whoever you are,
when you judge another; for in passing judgment upon
him you condemn yourself, because you, the judge, are
doing the very same things. We know that the judgment
of God rightly falls upon those who do such things. Do
you suppose, O man, that when you judge those who do
such things and yet do them yourself, you will escape the
judgment of God? Or do you presume upon the riches
of his kindness and forbearance and patience? Do you
not know that God's kindness is meant to lead you to repentance? But by your hard and impenitent heart you are
storing up wrath for yourself on the day of wrath when
God's righteous judgment will be revealed.*

After describing the avalanche of sin resulting from
separation from God, Paul — knowing that we tend
to see mainly the sins of others — points out that
the sins we see in them are but a reflection of our
own.

Our fault-finding betrays a false evaluation of
ourselves. We think we stand higher in God's esti-
mation than others do. I judge and condemn someone else for the very sin I have failed to see and deal

with in myself, not resisting it wholeheartedly. Whenever I am critical of others, this shows that I have not allowed God to judge me thoroughly on this point in my own life. Apart from spiritual blindness, another reason for a judgmental spirit is presumptuousness. We think it is possible for us to escape the judgment of God, imagining that God does not know what we are like.

As soon as we ask ourselves, 'What does God think of me?', we will stop finding fault with others. When we realize that all of us, without exception, must appear before the judgment seat of Christ (2 Corinthians 5:10), where the whole of our sinful nature will be laid bare, we will no longer judge others. God challenges us to accept His kindness as a call to repent and mend our ways. For it is only the kindness of God that He does not immediately punish us with spiritual death, as we deserve because of our sins. He patiently waits for our change of heart; He gives us time to turn from our sins. Yet often we misinterpret God's patience, thinking that He does not take our sin seriously and that we can escape His judgment.

This is the greatest blindness. As a result of it, we continue to store up God's wrath for ourselves. Instead of judging the other person, I should step into the light of God, accepting His warning and submitting to His discipline. Then His wrath will not descend upon me on that day when His righteous judgment is revealed.

2:6-11
For he will render to every man according to his works:
to those who by patience in well-doing seek for glory and
honour and immortality, he will give eternal life; but for
those who are factious and do not obey the truth, but
obey wickedness, there will be wrath and fury. There will
be tribulation and distress for every human being who
does evil, the Jew first and also the Greek, but glory and
honour and peace for every one who does good, the Jew
first and also the Greek. For God shows no partiality.

God does not judge us by what we know. He is
concerned about what we do — whether we are
patiently doing good, seeking the eternal life that
He offers. This alone is pleasing to God. He knows
what we are like on the inside. It is not how much
we pray that matters to Him, but whether our
prayers produce the fruit of a life pleasing to Him.
Only then do we bring Him glory. God is honoured
and glorified, for instance, when we live in reconciliation, revealing a long-suffering love. By leading God-pleasing lives, we can also face the coming
time of testing with childlike trust and will experience the love of God and His all-pervasive peace
amid affliction.

2:12-18, 21
All who have sinned without the law will also perish
without the law, and all who have sinned under the law
will be judged by the law. For it is not the hearers of the
law who are righteous before God, but the doers of the

law who will be justified. When Gentiles who have not the law do by nature what the law requires, they are a law to themselves, even though they do not have the law. They show that what the law requires is written on their hearts, while their conscience also bears witness and their conflicting thoughts accuse or perhaps excuse them on that day when, according to my gospel, God judges the secrets of men by Christ Jesus.

But if you call yourself a Jew and rely upon the law and boast of your relation to God and know his will and approve what is excellent, because you are instructed in the law . . . you then who teach others, will you not teach yourself?

God has revealed His moral law to everyone — not only to the Jews but also to the Gentiles. So for everyone it is a matter of wanting to do what His law commands and actually doing it. This poses a question for us: Do we live up to what we know?

Jesus saved us so that we would bring forth fruit by what we do. Now He asks us, 'Have you appropriated My redemption? Have you laid hold of it so thoroughly that you are really giving Me love and honour?' Everyone has the chance of accepting Jesus' salvation. For both Jewish and Gentile Christians, Jesus is Judge as well as merciful Lord.

2:19-24
. . . and if you are sure that you are a guide to the blind, a light to those who are in darkness, a corrector of the

foolish, a teacher of children, having in the law the embodiment of knowledge and truth — you then who teach others, will you not teach yourself? While you preach against stealing, do you steal? You who say that one must not commit adultery, do you commit adultery? You who abhor idols, do you rob temples? You who boast in the law, do you dishonour God by breaking the law? For, as it is written, 'The name of God is blasphemed among the Gentiles because of you.'

Those in charge of the flock are in particular danger of becoming self-righteous, thinking they are better than others. The more we are blessed by God with spiritual knowledge, the greater is the danger of hypocrisy and of becoming inwardly hardened. Again and again we must ask ourselves, 'Do I really submit to His judgment and thus come under His grace? Or do I enjoy preaching to others and exhorting them, without realizing that I am just as bad?'

Paul cannot emphasize enough that God's holiness is pure light, which shows us more and more clearly, the nearer we draw to Him, what sinners we are — rotten through and through. If we think our knowledge of biblical truths makes us better than others and gives us the right to teach them, we are for this very reason an abomination to God. If we speak piously and yet fail to do God's will, we bring disgrace on God. This is why God's holy name is often more dishonoured by us Christians than by atheists. We often cause Him more grief than the world in its sin.

2:25-29

Circumcision indeed is of value if you obey the law; but if you break the law, your circumcision becomes uncircumcision. So, if a man who is uncircumcised keeps the precepts of the law, will not his uncircumcision be regarded as circumcision? Then those who are physically uncircumcised but keep the law will condemn you who have the written code and circumcision but break the law. For he is not a real Jew who is one outwardly, nor is true circumcision something external and physical. He is a Jew who is one inwardly, and real circumcision is a matter of the heart, spiritual and not literal. His praise is not from men but from God.

Paul clearly demonstrates that being circumcised means nothing if we do not obey God's laws. God seeks in each one of us the circumcision of the heart (Deuteronomy 10:16). Without this all else is futile. The circumcision of the heart, however, is a painful process, involving the cutting out of sin, just as the vine needs to be pruned (John 15). Time and again the Lord has to prune us, but we must be willing to allow Him. Circumcision for the Jews and, even more so, baptism for New Testament believers are God's gracious offers. They are not to be effected merely outwardly, but need to take place inwardly as a true 'circumcision of the heart'. We can appear to accept God's gracious offers, without actually allowing them to bring about a change in our lives. According to Luther, baptism means 'that our sinful self, with all its evil deeds and desires, should be drowned through daily repentance; and that day after day a new self should arise to live with God in righteousness and purity for ever' (*The Small Catechism*).

We often assume that it is enough for our sins to be covered by the grace of God, without our actually being willing to make a break with sin. We are reluctant to put our self-love to death and to sacrifice our ego.

We have little idea how much God wants our sinful nature to be pruned and purified. Because of His great mercy to us, He wants us to offer ourselves as a living sacrifice, a holy sacrifice acceptable to Him (Romans 12:1). He wants us to fulfil His law, His commandment to love Him with all our hearts and our neighbour as ourselves (Matthew 22:37-39).

Fulfilling a commandment of God just outwardly is vastly different from fulfilling it in love and thus in truth. When God begins to measure us by His holy, divine standards, all our excuses are silenced and we can only confess, 'I am guilty in the sight of God.' Yet how difficult it is for us to come to the point of really confessing our sin and guilt in definite terms before God and man!

ROMANS
— THREE —

3:1-8

Then what advantage has the Jew? Or what is the value of circumcision? Much in every way. To begin with, the Jews are entrusted with the oracles of God. What if some were unfaithful? Does their faithlessness nullify the faithfulness of God? By no means! Let God be true though every man be false, as it is written, 'That thou mayest be justified in thy words, and prevail when thou art judged.' But if our wickedness serves to show the justice of God, what shall we say? That God is unjust to inflict wrath on us? (I speak in a human way.) By no means! For then how could God judge the world? But if through my falsehood God's truthfulness abounds to his glory, why am I still being condemned as a sinner? And why not do evil that good may come? — as some people slanderously charge us with saying. Their condemnation is just.

Not wishing anyone to miss out on the precious gift of God's grace, Paul patiently tackles the objections, although it is like boring a hole in a slab of granite.

Even if the ceremonies are not enough — in this case, circumcision, put forward by the Jewish Christians for discussion — God still works through these outward signs. His faithfulness is not put off by the unfaithfulness of those who have made themselves independent and rely on their own righteousness. God stands by His saving purposes. In view of such faithfulness, those who are honest can only humble themselves before the holiness of God, realizing that everything we receive from God is sheer grace. The insincere conclude: 'If my unrighteousness actually enhances God's faithfulness, how can He condemn me for my sinfulness?' Perhaps we do not express it so bluntly; yet this is our attitude. We think we can manipulate God, treating Him like a lifeless object. But my sin always grieves God deeply, even if it glorifies His faithfulness by throwing it into sharp relief. How evil it is, therefore, to conclude: 'Now I can safely go on sinning!' Ultimately, it all depends on our relationship to Him. Do we regard Him as a personal or impersonal God?

3:9-18

What then? Are we Jews any better off? No, not at all; for I have already charged that all men, both Jews and Greeks, are under the power of sin, as it is written: 'None is righteous, no, not one; no one understands, no one seeks for God. All have turned aside, together they have gone wrong; no one does good, not even one.' 'Their throat is an open grave, they use their tongues to deceive.' 'The venom of asps is under their lips.' 'Their mouth is full of curses and bitterness.' 'Their feet are swift to shed blood, in their paths are ruin and misery, and the way of peace they do not know.' 'There is no fear of God before their eyes.'

It is not by chance that from Romans 1:18 to 3:20 Paul writes in detail about our need to admit our guilt before the holiness of God, being genuinely appalled at our condition. To admit that I myself am guilty goes against my human nature, especially when I consider myself to be a devout Christian. I defend, perhaps unconsciously, my 'good qualities' to the hilt. However, we have to face up to reality: 'All have turned aside.' We are all rebels against Him, our Maker and Redeemer. 'No one does good, not even one' (3:12).

All our deeds — though ethically good — are worth nothing in God's sight. Only the grace of God can produce good in us — provided that we recognize ourselves as sinners. Our human blood is corrupt through and through. Even when we try to keep the law of God, we are not prompted by fear of God. God is not interested in such endeavours. What really matters to Him is that we keep His commandments of love, so that we might be truly righteous in His sight as His beloved children, who love Him above all else.

3:19-20

Now we know that whatever the law says it speaks to those who are under the law, so that every mouth may be stopped, and the whole world may be held accountable to God. For no human being will be justified in his sight by works of the law, since through the law comes knowledge of sin.

Instead of loving God, we continually try to present Him with our own achievements. How wrong this striving is! In one way or another, we try to bargain with God. But it grieves Him when we treat Him like a partner in a business deal and try to justify ourselves through 'good deeds'. Then we are not acting as His children. The more we try to fulfil His law in our own strength, the more we actually oppose God, being blind to our sins.

God does not want us to try and fulfil the law in our own strength, for we could not anyway. His desire is that the law will prompt us to take the first step towards Him. Measured against the standard of His law, the immensity of our sin dawns on us. We find ourselves failing to fulfil the law and thus exposed to the wrath of God. But then the law — acting as our tutor (Galatians 3:24 RAV) — leads us to Christ. In Him we find refuge from the divine wrath, because in His compassion He has come to our aid. Though rejection of God's will is deeply ingrained in our human nature, Christ has transformed that rejection into loving obedience — by His atoning death.

3:21-22
But now the righteousness of God apart from the law is revealed, being witnessed by the Law and the Prophets,

even the righteousness of God which is through faith in
Jesus Christ to all and on all who believe. (RAV)

'But now!' Paul goes on to say, stopping us in our
tracks. Another way to be accepted by God has
been laid open for us — something totally different
from legalistically observing the law. Justification
is offered as a free gift of His grace through the ransom paid by Christ Jesus (3:24). We are declared
righteous in the sight of God through faith in Jesus
Christ and in His atoning sacrifice (3:22). This is the
firm foundation on which we stand.

The commandments of God given at Mount
Sinai reveal His love, for it is an act of grace that He
should speak to us sinful human beings at all and
show us what He wants of us. Jesus' cry at Calvary,
'It is finished!' expresses an even greater love:
through the sacrifice of Jesus Christ, God's righteousness is fulfilled in us — if we have faith in our
Saviour.

Mount Sinai represents the holiness of God,
whereas Calvary stands for His grace. Jesus Christ
paid a high price for our redemption when He took
our place and bore the punishment for our sins.
Through His agony in Gethsemane, His path of
sorrows and bitter death on the cross, the righteousness of God comes to us and we are justified.
God in His holiness cannot be approached by us.
But in Jesus Christ He comes to us and actually
lives in us. Because of our sinful nature, all our
endeavours to keep the law are frustrated; but in

Jesus we can cling to God in faith, and so receive His righteousness.

It is a token of God's love that He gave us the law. Without the law we would deceive ourselves into thinking that our standards are acceptable to God and that we can meet Him on our own terms. The law in its absoluteness and holiness shows up our imagined human greatness as worthless. Now by faith in Jesus Christ we receive the righteousness of God (3:21-22). His holy will proclaimed at Sinai is fulfilled in us by the grace of Calvary. But first we need to taste the holiness of God and thus His wrath. We need to realize that we are nothing but guilty before Him (3:19). This is the only way that His grace can gain room in us through Jesus Christ and that a new life in righteousness can begin.

God's righteousness will be turned into saving grace for us to the extent that we accept His judgment. Grace corresponds to judgment. First, we need to recognize the judgment of God — when He admonishes us in our consciences, or chastens us through suffering or through the way others treat us. Instead of trying to evade the issue, we should face up to God's judgment, being broken before Him and humbly admitting our failure to keep His holy commandments. This way, we would not persist in being complacent and self-righteous, pampering our sinful nature. If we are willing to be judged for our sins — for instance, our fault-finding or lack of love — and are always ready to admit our failings, then we are really appropriating Jesus' righteousness.

This is how the amazing gift of God's righteousness gains increasing room in us. It is a question of whether we are willing to be convicted of our sin, not just once but day by day, because Jesus' righteousness comes to us only in so far as we submit to His holiness. Then He pours out His grace upon us. Submitting to God's righteousness in judgment is a painful experience. But the more we do so, the more He will free us from our chains of sin, by His grace. Righteousness is available for us all — without distinction — provided we really want it and receive it in faith. Faith, however, is inseparable from the humble admission that 'all have sinned', including ourselves.

3:22-24

There is no difference; for all have sinned and fall short of the glory of God, being justified freely by His grace through the redemption that is in Christ Jesus ... (RAV)

The conclusion 'all have sinned' goes against our pride. We either have a superiority complex or — out of despondency, which stems from pride — suffer from an inferiority complex. But the only way to escape the terrible wrath of God is to accept wholeheartedly the verdict 'all have sinned' — including ourselves. It's up to us. Are we willing to submit to God and to see ourselves as sinners? If we long for grace with all our hearts, He will justify us through the free gift of His grace, without any merit on our part.

If we have not experienced His grace, the reason is that we did not really want it. The fact that we receive so little grace invariably reveals our *No* to it. We should desire grace with our whole being. We will only receive the fullness of grace when in every situation we look first to see where we are the one at fault. If we become aware of our own guilt and stand humbled before others, we will be able to receive the grace of God. Satan, however, is right at our heels, determined to snatch away from us the precious gift of grace, which Jesus procured for us through His salvation. The evil one is plotting and scheming the whole time to win us for himself through our self-righteousness or despondency. But God has intervened for everyone in the person of Jesus Christ, who has redeemed us from Satan's captivity. This holds true for all who believe.

3:25-26
. . . whom God set forth to be a propitiation by His blood, through faith, to demonstrate His righteousness, because in His forbearance God had passed over the sins that were previously committed, to demonstrate at the present time His righteousness, that He might be just and the justifier of the one who has faith in Jesus. (RAV)

How does redemption come to us? The godlessness (chapter 1) and the self-righteousness (chapter

2) of all generations have been crying out to heaven. Then Jesus became the atoning sacrifice (propitiation of sin), taking upon Himself the punishment of God, which all the world deserved because of its self-righteousness. The judgment that should have fallen upon us fell upon Jesus instead: the holy wrath of God. God inflicted the punishment upon Jesus, granting us grace in exchange. For this we can never thank Him enough. So let us love Him fervently, placing our whole lives at His disposal.

What must it have meant for Jesus to bear the sins of us all! What agony to take upon Himself the full wrath of God! And yet, what good news the sufferings of Jesus bring to us! Through His death on the cross we are offered the righteousness of God. My sins are condemned by God in the death of Jesus, and at the same time God releases me from the yoke of sin. The judgment that Jesus suffered for us on the cross has delivered us from the misery of sin and from eternal damnation. Out of gratitude may our hearts be ever devoted to Him in love.

When we are at the end of our own resources, Jesus offers us, by His blood, forgiveness for all our sins. He is our throne of grace, or mercy seat, foreshadowed by the one in the Holy of Holies in the Temple. (The Ark of the Covenant containing the Ten Commandments was covered by the mercy seat, which protected the people from the holiness of God expressed in the law.) When we believe in

Jesus and put all our trust in Him, God justifies us — even though we don't deserve to be justified! We must not despair, nor should we rely on cheap grace. In both instances our ego is at the centre. We presumptuously think we can fulfil God's will in our own strength; or else we are indifferent and tolerate sin in our lives, thus misusing Jesus' salvation. But He Himself wants to transform our lives, so that we bow down before Him, acknowledging Him as our great love. God does not demand that we produce something out of ourselves to please Him. Righteousness is what He looks for in us. And He alone effects it in us through grace, when we cling in faith to Jesus and to His atoning sacrifice for us.

3:27

Then what becomes of our boasting? It is excluded. On what principle? On the principle of works? No, but on the principle of faith.

There is no more pride of achievement. All we are left with is pain because of our sin and a sense of awe and wonder at the grace of His forgiveness. When we experience His forgiveness, we all find ourselves on the same level — as sinners in need of grace. Fault-finding and feelings of superiority have no place any longer. It is here that His followers are truly united, because they have something in common — in faith looking to Him alone for newness of life. People do not follow Jesus *en masse*, drawn together because of the same way of thinking; only penitent sinners meet beneath His cross. Every division among Christians is removed when they live in true repentance, trusting in the forgiving love of Jesus, the Friend of sinners.

3:28
For we hold that a man is justified by faith apart from works of law.

Faith is not passive, as might appear here at first glance, but thoroughly active. In contrast, legalism is merely a show of religion and only outwardly active. Faith brings us the great privilege of living more and more in the holy presence of God. If we realize that we are justified by faith alone and count on God working in our hearts and lives, we will increasingly see what sinners we are.

There is no one who is too weak or too sinful to practise such faith consistently day by day. Thanks to the great mercy of God, we do not have to produce a life that is faultless. We need only admit what we are really like. We are saved not by the good things we do but rather by trusting in what God has done for us. The result is that we have a wonderful and unexpected open door to Jesus Christ, who makes us righteous when we trust in Him.

3:29-31
Or is God the God of Jews only? Is he not the God of Gentiles also? Yes, of Gentiles also, since God is one; and he will justify the circumcised on the ground of their faith and the uncircumcised through their faith. Do we then overthrow the law by this faith? By no means! On the contrary, we uphold the law.

Aren't we actually turning aside from the law with this attitude? Not at all! The law convicts us of our helplessness and drives us to Jesus Christ. He sets us free to do His will and so fulfil the law, as we trust in His saving power at work in us. Faith does not rob the law of its force, rather it gives the law its true value (3:31). So let us pray, 'Lord, give me light, and by Your blood release me from my sins, which oppose the law.' If I pray constantly for light about myself and release from my sinful nature, I will experience this.

The question is: Do I prefer to cling to my sins, not having recognized self for what it is, nor having learnt to hate it? Or am I really willing to be freed from my resentment, my self-will, my judgmental spirit? Our answer should be: I want to persevere in faith as a sign to the Lord that I am His. Then He will justify us through our faith and we will be increasingly able to fulfil the law, His commandments.

ROMANS
— FOUR —

4:1-8
What then shall we say about Abraham, our forefather according to the flesh? For if Abraham was justified by works, he has something to boast about, but not before God. For what does the scripture say? 'Abraham believed God, and it was reckoned to him as righteousness.' Now to one who works, his wages are not reckoned as a gift but as his due. And to one who does not work but trusts him who justifies the ungodly, his faith is reckoned as righteousness. So also David pronounces a blessing upon the man to whom God reckons righteousness apart from works: 'Blessed are those whose iniquities are forgiven, and whose sins are covered; blessed is the man against whom the Lord will not reckon his sin.'

Over Abraham's life the words can be written 'by faith alone'. To others he could have boasted of his obedience in leaving his native land and his relatives, but not before God, since everything God gives us is grace. Abraham received an heir only because he put his faith in God. Looking up at the countless stars in the sky, he believed — against all human expectations — that his descendants would be just as numerous. Why? Because God had said so. We, too, are to have implicit faith that Jesus Christ is transforming us and that the immeasurable gap between God and us has been bridged by Him. As Abraham looked at the starry sky, he was filled with love for his Maker. Similarly, we should be moved by love to put our whole trust in our Lord Jesus Christ and to rely on His salvation.

Abraham knew that in the sight of God he was ungodly. He saw that he was wrong to have had doubts about the promise of an heir. He recognized that God alone is wise and just. For this reason he was in the best possible position to put his faith in God. He expected nothing of himself, but everything of God, who 'justifies the ungodly'. This involves living in a state of tension between believing and seeing, a struggle that has to be endured. I need to admit that I am ungodly, in every way blameworthy, without excuse; and at the same time I need to trust that God is doing a miracle and making me, the ungodly one, righteous.

True joy in God comes from seeing myself again and again in daily life as a sinner. Instead of suppressing my sins or explaining them away, I admit where I have failed and gone wrong. Then I come to appreciate the wonder of Jesus' atoning death for me and of the forgiveness of my sins through Him. Without my doing anything to deserve it, His righteousness is credited to me, and 'Christ in us' becomes a reality in my life. All our human guilt is far exceeded by the greatness of His forgiveness. When we admit our sins and in faith receive forgiveness, they are wiped out. Our faith is regarded by God as righteousness.

'There is no saint that did not lament his unholiness and weep over his sins' (Luther). This is true of the life of King David. David's sin of adultery became public knowledge, because he openly admitted his sin. Even today he can still point people to God, for his psalms continue to comfort and help those who feel the burden of their sin:

> Deliver me from bloodguiltiness, O God, thou
> God of my salvation, and my tongue will sing
> aloud of thy deliverance . . . For thou hast no
> delight in sacrifice; were I to give a burnt offering, thou wouldst not be pleased. The sacrifice
> acceptable to God is a broken spirit; a broken
> and contrite heart, O God, thou wilt not despise
> (Psalm 51:14-17).

4:9-12

Is this blessing pronounced only upon the circumcised, or also upon the uncircumcised? We say that faith was reckoned to Abraham as righteousness. How then was it reckoned to him? Was it before or after he had been circumcised? It was not after, but before he was circumcised. He received circumcision as a sign or seal of the righteousness which he had by faith while he was still uncircumcised. The purpose was to make him the father of all who believe without being circumcised and who thus have righteousness reckoned to them, and likewise the father of the circumcised who are not merely circum-

cised but also follow the example of the faith which our father Abraham had before he was circumcised.

God has made grace available to all, to the circumcised and the uncircumcised alike. He grants grace to those who were consecrated to Him by circumcision in accordance with the Old Covenant, and also to those who were not included in the covenant — the uncircumcised, the Gentile nations. The way of faith is open to all. There are no pre-conditions.

In the Old Covenant this fact is established by God's dealings with Abraham. He was praised not because he was circumcised (4:9-10), but because he trusted God to intervene in his life and to give to him who had no children as many descendants as there are stars in the sky. Abraham's circumcision was a seal, a seal of authenticity, upon the righteousness God had credited to him for his faith. Faith is what counts, not circumcision as an outward sign. By believing God, a man was circumcised in the true sense and so really belonged to the people of God (2:29).

Circumcision can be practised as a ritual on a purely human level. But human acts and achievements make no impression on God. He looks for a faith that reaches out for the redemption He has provided. He seeks this faith in us, in order to put us right with Him. When Abraham believed, God justified him on account of his faith. Living by faith means trusting in God's gracious provision in our spiritual poverty. It means believing that His grace is far greater and deeper than we can imagine.

Do you ever wonder, 'Am I rejected after all?' 'Does His offer of grace apply to me too?' 'Does it still hold good?' Then you may rest assured: His grace does avail for you. The grace of God is greater than our burden of sin. Whether we are weak or strong is irrelevant. God bestows His grace on all provided that we do not reject grace by proudly seeking to be justified by good works done in our own strength.

4:13-16

For the promise that he would be the heir of the world was not to Abraham or to his seed through the law, but through the righteousness of faith. For if those who are of the law are heirs, faith is made void and the promise made of no effect, because the law brings about wrath; for where there is no law there is no transgression. Therefore it is of faith that it might be according to grace, so that the promise might be sure to all the seed, not only to those who are of the law, but also to those who are of the faith of Abraham, who is the father of us all . . . (RAV)

Abraham's seed was to inherit the world through faith. In him all the nations of the earth were to be blessed (Genesis 18:18), and his descendants were to be co-heirs of an abiding city, built according to the design and by the working of God (Hebrews 11:10). Such a promise was made to Abraham on account of the righteousness of faith, and not because he would ever have been capable of fulfilling the law in his own strength (4:13-14). If we try to win God's blessing and salvation through legalism, even demanding a reward by boasting about our achievements, then none of the glorious promises of God can materialize. God can give blessings only to those who have no demands to make — the ungodly, the powerless, those who are capable of nothing but believing in the grace of God and trusting Him to accomplish in them what they cannot do themselves. Before God can fulfil promises in our lives, He has to break our pride, so that we don't stand in His way with the high opinion we have of ourselves.

This happens when we see we are unable to fulfil the law's demands on us. Then we are driven to Jesus Christ, the mercy seat. Without Christ, the law leads to ego-boosting, pride and Pharisaism, thus bringing on us the wrath of God. But a transformation takes place when we rely on Jesus, when we trust that His vicarious suffering and His atoning death give us righteousness. He awakens in us the desire to fulfil His will in the power of His sacrifice. He can give us a contrite heart and make us willing to accept our cross in everyday life as coming from Him. Instead of rejecting our cross, we then bear it for love of our Lord, who will take care that it won't be too heavy.

The promises given to Abraham point to Jesus (Galatians 3:16). By faith in Him we are able to do what is otherwise impossible for us. Without faith in Him, everything is limited to self-effort. For instance, for fear of saying the wrong thing, we may make up our minds not to say anything at all. We may even pride ourselves on our silence, not noticing how hard-hearted and unloving we are being. When we act in our own strength, we are always boosting our ego rather than humbling ourselves and becoming more like Jesus in His lowliness (Philippians 2:5, 8). This is why Paul fought passionately against all human asceticism. It is poison. It traps us in 'justification by works'. We end up with the law without the mercy seat, without Jesus' salvation.

So when we are unmasked before ourselves and others in our questionable actions and false motives, we can only thank the Lord. Then we will cling even more to the truth that we are justified only through faith in our Saviour Jesus Christ (3:28), and not by any good deeds we do. Only when I surrender my human striving to Jesus, asking Him to take away all my self-effort and to give me instead a contrite and broken heart, only then will He grant me newness of life. For example, He makes me more compassionate in dealing with difficult people — by showing me that my personality problems are as slow in changing as theirs. Being merciful with one another through Christ is a mark of righteousness by grace. So we need feel neither superior nor ashamed before each other. That is a gift of His forgiveness.

4:16-22

*. . . for he [Abraham] is the father of us all, as it is writ-
ten, 'I have made you the father of many nations' — in
the presence of the God in whom he believed, who gives
life to the dead and calls into existence the things that do
not exist. In hope he believed against hope, that he
should become the father of many nations; as he had been
told, 'So shall your descendants be.' He did not weaken
in faith when he considered his own body, which was as
good as dead because he was about a hundred years old,
or when he considered the barrenness of Sarah's womb.
No distrust made him waver concerning the promise of
God, but he grew strong in his faith as he gave glory to
God, fully convinced that God was able to do what he
had promised. That is why his faith was 'reckoned to him
as righteousness.'*

Abraham walked by faith. He knew what it was
like to be utterly helpless in oneself. Yet he believed
that God has the power to call into existence the
things that do not exist. He believed that God
could call forth life in Sarah's barren womb. He
also believed that, since God is able to make the
dead come alive, He could preserve Isaac, in spite
of commanding Abraham to offer him as a sacrifice. In the final analysis, Abraham focused on the
Saviour Jesus Christ in everything (John 8:56). This
is what faith is all about: After seeing what I am
like, not getting bogged down by my sins but looking away, clinging to God's Word and faithfulness,
to the redemption and victory of Jesus. In this great

tension we have to remain, never trying to escape it.

When our sinful nature is exposed, we need to turn our backs on doubt and to look to Jesus instead. We have to practise this kind of faith till our last breath. Reason, which argues that we will never be freed from the yoke of our sin, must yield to faith: God will accomplish what He has purposed. We can joyfully look forward to actually becoming all that God has in mind for us to be. Christ has given us a holy calling (2 Timothy 1:9). We are challenged to take hold of eternal life (1 Timothy 6:12). It is vital that we cling to this promise, that we do not waver in faith. Then God will fulfil His promise.

When we suffer anguish because we can sense how strong our chains of sin are, let us hold fast to this: Just as God gives life to the dead, He will grant us more and more of His resurrection life, that is, victory over sin. If we are faithful in this battle, we will be able to see Him one day as overcomers. 'He who conquers . . .' — this is the theme of the Letters to the Seven Churches in Asia Minor (Revelation 2 and 3). 'He who conquers, I will grant him to sit with me on my throne' (Revelation 3:21).

4:23-25
But the words, 'it was reckoned to him,' were written not for his sake alone, but for ours also. It will be reckoned to us who believe in him that raised from the dead

Jesus our Lord, who was put to death for our trespasses and raised for our justification.

Abraham's story is continually being repeated. Through faith people are receiving life and victory from God. We, too, are called to believe as Abraham did — without seeing. When there seems to be no way out, we need to trust in the omnipotence of the Father and rely on our Lord Jesus Christ, who at Calvary cried out victoriously, 'It is finished!'

Yet how quickly we grow discouraged and become rebels, blaming God when release from self is not as fast as we were expecting. If, however, we really believe that God has given His Son for us and that in Him we have all we need, then we continue to wait patiently. We have the assurance that He will give us victory in His own time. In Jesus Christ, God loves us with an everlasting love. This knowledge is our confidence as we battle in faith against sin. It is also our hope for the difficult time of testing ahead. Not merely now but then as well, God will prove to be a refuge for His children, for whom He has done marvellous things, freeing them from the grip of Satan and making them His own possession. Such paths of faith not only release us from self, but they also glorify God and magnify His name.

ROMANS
—— FIVE ——

5:1-4

Therefore, since we are justified by faith, we have peace with God through our Lord Jesus Christ. Through him we have obtained access to this grace in which we stand, and we rejoice in our hope of sharing the glory of God. More than that, we rejoice in our sufferings, knowing that suffering produces endurance, and endurance produces character, and character produces hope.

If I look to Christ for salvation, then I have peace with God. As soon as I have no peace with God, this is a sign that I am tolerating sin in my life instead of bringing it to Jesus to be forgiven and cleansed by His blood. If I refuse to let the Lord convict me of sin, I miss out on His grace as well. If I don't bring my sins to Jesus in contrition, they cannot be forgiven and blotted out by His blood. I end up rebelling against circumstances and against people, who either point out my mistakes or show me up by their conduct. In this state I am living for self, asserting my self-righteousness and self-will. Consequently, I lose the peace I had with God.

Having peace with God means being willing to accept reproof and correction in everyday life out of gratitude to my crucified Lord. Then I experience the reality of His grace as He forgives me my specific sins. As soon as I stop defending my own righteousness, my correctness, my rights, my reputation, and instead surrender myself entirely to God, my life is filled with peace. Having peace with God means saying *Yes* wholeheartedly to God's dealings with me, even when He uses people as His instruments. Then, come what may, I retain this peace with God — through faith. It is a matter of continually reaching out for His peace.

So we rejoice in our hope — not the hope in a new social order, which will eventually pass away, but the hope in a future glory, which is imperishable. There will be no more inner conflict, and all sadness will melt away; for, transformed into His image, we will see Him. We will be allowed to share the glory and radiance of our Lord. It is His love which implants in our hearts this longing for the heavenly glory and for union with Him.

Through our Lord Jesus Christ we can even rejoice in the midst of afflictions, difficulties, disappointments, perils and every other kind of suffering. Why is this? It is a spiritual law that troubles teach us to endure patiently in faith. By nature we resist afflictions: we dislike bearing burdens. But under the pressure of suffering, faith rises to the challenge. Trials and temptations are meant to teach us to persevere in faith, to practise patience and faithfulness to God. Afflictions help to produce these qualities in us.

God gives us suffering so as to release us from self, which dominates our thoughts and actions. He longs for us to turn to Him and make Him the centre of our lives. This is exemplified in the story of Job. In Job's life God even had to use Satan until Job learnt to cry out to his Lord, and God finally heard from Job's lips the confession, 'I despise myself, and repent in dust and ashes' (Job 42:6). God intervenes in our lives with chastening, so that we will come to see our sin and admit it. He leads us through deep inner conflict to deal with our pride, so that we will learn patience and steadfast endurance, setting our hope increasingly on Him alone. All the time His desire is to prepare us for the Marriage Supper of the Lamb.

5:5
Now hope does not disappoint us, because the love of God has been poured out in our hearts by the Holy Spirit who was given to us. (RAV)

Paul explains why faith bears such great fruit: God's love has been poured into our hearts. It is the love of Jesus Christ, which the Holy Spirit reveals to us. He opens our eyes to see how greatly Jesus loves us. And anyone who has experienced the love of Jesus is compelled to trust in Him. For love of his Lord he accepts everything that happens to him, no matter how great the suffering may be that God brings into his life.

5:6-9

While we were yet helpless, at the right time Christ died for the ungodly. Why, one will hardly die for a righteous man — though perhaps for a good man one will dare even to die. But God shows his love for us in that while we were yet sinners Christ died for us. Since, therefore, we are now justified by his blood, much more shall we be saved by him from the wrath of God.

Because we are weak, powerless to help ourselves, Christ died for us, the ungodly, 'at the right time' — the time God chose. For our sakes the Son of the Everlasting Father suffered the crucifixion. Now He wants the power of His death and resurrection to become effective in our lives. Help often comes when we are not expecting it, but the timing is always right. After a long and seemingly hopeless struggle with sin, release and victory will come 'at the right time'. We may have battled in faith a long time, but the Lord alone decides the moment of victory.

What love God has shown in letting Christ die for us, the ungodly! How much it must have cost the holy God! Because God is love, He made this sacrifice for us. The Son of the Everlasting Father took the place of us sinners when He died. We can grasp this miracle only if we see ourselves as sinners — and not just once but again and again. If we somehow regard ourselves as better than 'ungodly', we have no idea of what Jesus' atoning sacrifice really means. Instead of becoming seeing

people in His light, we are blind. Satan is at work
here. He repeatedly tries to discredit the great miracle of Jesus Christ, the only begotten Son of God,
dying for the ungodly. Despondency is his
weapon.

Despondency is an expression of boundless
pride. We cannot bear to think that we have sinned
and failed again. If we did see ourselves as lost
souls, 'ungodly' by nature, we wouldn't be sur-
prised at what we are like. Our attitude towards
others would be different, too. If we can't get on
with someone, we would blame ourselves, saying,
'I am like the man with the log in his eye; the other
person is the one with the speck' (see Matthew 7:3).
But we are too proud to come to the foot of the
cross every day anew to receive God's grace and
then go our way as pardoned sinners.

Yet the love of God was never so clearly
expressed as when Christ died for us sinners to
save us from the eternal wrath we deserve. If we
face up to our sinfulness and at the same time reach
out for His love in faith, then one day we will be
able to face the all-revealing light of Jesus confi-
dently and without fear.

5:10-11
*For if while we were enemies we were reconciled to God
by the death of his Son, much more, now that we are reconciled, shall we be saved by his life. Not only so, but we
also rejoice in God through our Lord Jesus Christ,
through whom we have now received our reconciliation.*

Though by nature alienated from God, we have truly been reconciled to the Almighty, who will one day judge the living and the dead. While we were still His enemies, God in His love brought about this transformation through Jesus' death for us. How thankful we can be that Jesus, as the Son of God, not only died but rose for us! By His victory over sin and death we are delivered from sin's dominion. Paul is a jubilant witness to this. Yes, through Jesus we are actually released from our sinful bonds, and this release will be manifested in our lives bit by bit.

Even in human relationships there is distress and sadness when people are estranged. But imagine living in a permanent state of hostility to God. Because we are now reconciled through our Lord Jesus Christ, we need no longer fear such a prospect. Through Jesus' atoning sacrifice, the love of God embraces us both here and for ever in the heavenly glory.

5:12-21

Therefore as sin came into the world through one man and death through sin, and so death spread to all men because all men sinned — sin indeed was in the world before the law was given, but sin is not counted where there is no law. Yet death reigned from Adam to Moses, even over those whose sins were not like the transgression of Adam, who was a type of the one who was to come.

But the free gift is not like the trespass. For if many

died through one man's trespass, much more have the grace of God and the free gift in the grace of that one man Jesus Christ abounded for many. And the free gift is not like the effect of that one man's sin. For the judgment following one trespass brought condemnation, but the free gift following many trespasses brings justification. If, because of one man's trespass, death reigned through that one man, much more will those who receive the abundance of grace and the free gift of righteousness reign in life through the one man Jesus Christ.

Then as one man's trespass led to condemnation for all men, so one man's act of righteousness leads to acquittal and life for all men. For as by one man's disobedience many were made sinners, so by one man's obedience many will be made righteous. Law came in, to increase the trespass; but where sin increased, grace abounded all the more, so that, as sin reigned in death, grace also might reign through righteousness to eternal life through Jesus Christ our Lord.

Through Jesus Christ righteousness and life triumph over sin and death. Sin came into the world through Adam. When Adam — led astray by Eve and ultimately by Satan — succumbed to temptation, he didn't sin just for himself. By his act of disobedience he opened the gates of hell for all humanity. This is the reason why we must all die one day. Death is the sign that the whole world is under the rule of sin.

Adam was guilty of sin only because a command of God already existed, and to infringe it meant death. We must all die, because sin lives in us all and because, although we have the commandments of God, our natural preference is to sin. Yet the amazing grace imparted to us through the second Adam, our Saviour Jesus Christ, is out of all proportion to what Adam did and to what we all carry within us as the seed of death. Through Jesus we have received the fullness of grace and the free gift of righteousness, leading to eternal life.

Our Lord Jesus came not only to restore us to our condition before the Fall but also to make us kings and priests (Revelation 1:6), who will one day be given authority to judge and reign (Revelation 20:4; 22:5). Not only has He reversed the curse, but He has blessed us abundantly. Not only are we to regain paradise, but we are to partake of the Marriage Supper of the Lamb. Jesus did not simply end a certain unfavourable condition. He did far more. He brought about a tremendous renewal of man. We are engrafted in Jesus Christ, who gives us life.

One single sin was responsible for the ruin of all people, but through Jesus all who receive God's gift of forgiveness will be declared righteous and made acceptable to Him. It is beyond comprehension: This one act of Jesus put everything right again. He suffered the penalty that would otherwise have meant eternal misery for us in the kingdom of darkness. Sin does not remain as such, but is blotted out, having been atoned for. Jesus Christ has made us righteous through His obedience. So we stand upon a firm foundation. Our sin has been put to death through Him, and He has claimed us for Himself, declaring, 'You are Mine!'

What about God's law now? If I take His law seriously, if I regard the Sermon on the Mount as binding on my life, the sin in me will be stirred up all the more in the face of God's holy requirements. The holier the standard, the more sins are revealed. Yet this induces me to pray all the more for His light and to be released by His blood. In this way I will be granted an ever greater measure of His grace, for the more I see my sinfulness, the more I see God's abounding grace forgiving me.

The more seriously I take God's commandments, the more I will experience the forgiveness and redemption of Jesus and be transformed into His image. Battling in faith against sin is not an end in itself: it prepares us for fellowship with Him at the Marriage Supper of the Lamb in the City of God.

ROMANS
—— SIX ——

6:1-14

What shall we say then? Are we to continue in sin that grace may abound? By no means! How can we who died to sin still live in it? Do you not know that all of us who have been baptized into Christ Jesus were baptized into his death? We were buried therefore with him by baptism into death, so that as Christ was raised from the dead by the glory of the Father, we too might walk in newness of life.

For if we have been united with him in a death like his, we shall certainly be united with him in a resurrection like his. We know that our old self was crucified with him so that the sinful body might be destroyed, and we might no longer be enslaved to sin. For he who has died is freed from sin. But if we have died with Christ, we believe that we shall also live with him. For we know that Christ being raised from the dead will never die again; death no longer has dominion over him. The death he died he died to sin, once for all, but the life he lives he lives to God. So you also must consider yourselves dead to sin and alive to God in Christ Jesus.

Let not sin therefore reign in your mortal bodies, to make you obey their passions. Do not yield your members to sin as instruments of wickedness, but yield your-

*selves to God as men who have been brought from death
to life, and your members to God as instruments of righteousness. For sin will have no dominion over you, since
you are not under law but under grace.*

The apostle Paul tackles the hypothetical question,
Why not persist in sin, seeing that grace is so abun-
dant and great? Anyone loving the Lord will dis-
miss such thoughts as absurd. For love of Him and
in thanksgiving for His sacrifice we are committed
to the crucified Lord. We no longer need be slaves
of sin — not since Jesus dealt with sin by paying the
death-penalty for us. The message rings out clearly:
We were buried with Christ by baptism into death
(6:4), united with Him in a death like His, crucified
with Him (6:5-8). Life as a member of the body of
Christ can be summed up as union with Him, complete identification. Consequently, there is no such
thing as discipleship at a distance. There is only a
life 'in Christ' and 'Christ in me', as is shown in the
allegory of the vine and branches in John 15.

Love like this, having united us with Christ, will
help us to see from Jesus' suffering and sacrifice
just what our old self deserves: death. But knowing
this is not enough. That helps us as little as if Jesus'
mighty act of redemption, through which our sinful
body can stop serving sin, had never taken place.
We need to face up honestly and personally to what
it cost Jesus to carry our sins in His body to the
cross. As the Holy Spirit gives us light, we will be
filled with sorrow at the harm we cause by our sin-

ful impulses, by vanity, selfish ambition and self-will, all of which are part of our fallen human nature.

Such a realization awakens in us the longing to do the very opposite of what we naturally desire. By nature we seek that which pleases our body: we try to protect ourselves against any burden or privation. But as soon as we see our body in the light of God, we will no longer want to yield to its sinful demands. Rather, we will now claim in faith that we have died with Christ (6:8) and that the power of our old sin-loving nature is destroyed (6:6).

The apostle Paul paints a vivid picture of what the Lamb of God has done: 'If we have died with Christ, we believe that we shall also live with him. For we know that Christ being raised from the dead will never die again; death no longer has dominion over him. The death he died he died to sin, once for all, but the life he lives he lives to God' (6:8-10). With these words Paul points emphatically to the cross of Calvary, as it stands rammed into the earth, the watershed in world history and, whether we realize it or not, the place of decision for every human being. Jesus' death upon the cross for our sins was a *one-time* event. The many thousands of animal sacrifices in the Temple at Jerusalem were ultimately ineffectual, although they were repeated year after year. They were merely symbolic. But when 'Christ died for us', this single offering and unique act of God's love brought about a radical change. For in Christ's death my sin is put to death in His body.

This could be expressed in picture language. Let's say I am on a high mountain range, where I could slip down on either side into a rift in the rocks. But if I have an experienced guide, I need have no fear of losing my footing, because I am tied to the guide's rope, and he holds me securely.

Similarly, Jesus holds us securely in His sacrifice. With His death on the cross our sin is put to death, for He has borne our sins in His body on the tree (1 Peter 2:24). With this saving act our life takes a new direction — not towards pain and sorrow, as at Adam's fall, but towards life and salvation, towards release from the control of sin, which saddens and depresses us and ruins our lives.

From this mighty demonstration of God's love comes Paul's great love for Jesus, his Saviour. Jesus has done *everything* for us. What a privilege to belong to Him and be able to live a new life in Him! This life is not dominated by earthly, sensuous, sinful instincts, nor is it aimless. We are called to be 'in Jesus Christ', who has effected this great change for all mankind and for my personal life. He included me and the whole of my sinful nature in His death. This means He lets me share in His victorious life, which has broken the power of sin (6:7-8).

After Paul has proclaimed this great act of salvation, there follows an imperative, a requirement, a command. He faces us with a weighty decision:

'So you also must consider yourselves dead to sin' (6:11).

Jesus' salvation is the turning-point for the whole world and for our personal lives. It is all-inclusive and all-sufficient. Jesus Christ, and He alone, the only begotten Son of God, was able to atone for our sin and to ransom us with His precious blood from Satan's captivity — just as people used to be redeemed from a debtor's prison. We were bought with a great price, 'not with perishable things such as silver or gold, but with the precious blood of Christ' (1 Peter 1:18-19). And so we really are free.

This freedom, however, is not brought about in us mechanically. The victorious sacrifice of the Lamb of God is not a deed which automatically works out in the world or in any one of us. Certainly, the saving love of God is evident at Calvary, as God reaches out to us, seeking to win us for Himself and to lead us into the freedom of God's children through Jesus' atoning death. He does not want to abandon us to Satan and destruction. Love, however, does not force us to accept anything against our will, but rather waits for the response of love on our part. This means we can only accept His salvation voluntarily as a gift. This is what the apostle means by saying: You must 'consider yourselves dead to sin' (6:11). In other words, accept this gift, take hold of it as belonging to you. Suppose I have just received a Bible in a particular translation I've been wanting for a long time. If I don't remove the wrapping, what good does it do me? None at all.

Redemption in Christ is infinitely greater than any other gift. But how little do we actually take hold of this offer of God's grace! We tend to overlook it. We may, with our intellect, acknowledge that we have received a gift, but in reality we do not claim it. This is why His sacrifice has so little effect on our lives. This is why it doesn't work like dynamite on our apathetic, hard and sinful nature. We shed no tears of contrition, because in our self-righteousness we neglect to claim the power of the blood of Jesus. As a result, greed or obstinacy or untruthfulness becomes more firmly established in us. Yet it is a matter of life and death that we lay hold of Jesus' all-sufficient sacrifice in faith. We do this when we take to heart the apostle's warning, 'So you also must consider yourselves dead to sin' (6:11). This means trust and believe that what you have been given is actually yours!

However, we don't really take this admonition seriously, although we seek release from the power of sin harassing us and although we long to be gentle and loving and to produce good fruit for God. Indeed, we would like to lead a Christ-filled life that is a testimony to others, as He expects of us. And so we try to give God a token of our love, denying ourselves certain pleasures and giving up things we used to value. But the more we try to step into His light and to study God's Word, the more we realize how far away we are from Him, how far removed from real life in Jesus, and how little we have experienced the transforming power of His sacrifice. New life in Him is not imparted to us through doing this or through refraining from that. It comes through claiming in faith what He has obtained for us at Calvary. Despite all appearances and despite the reality that confronts us, we need to believe firmly: I have been united with Christ in a death like His.

Persevering in faith and standing our ground: this is the essence of our life with Jesus Christ. Thus the apostle Paul does not say at the end of his life, 'I have practised love; I have served the Lord; I have sacrificed myself', although there was much for which he could have taken credit. Rather, he says, 'I have kept the faith. Henceforth there is laid up for me the crown of righteousness' (2 Timothy 4:7-8). To hold on in faith to the fact that Christ personally carried the load of my sins in His own body when He died on the cross — that is the issue.

We need to practise a faith like this, especially when tempted to despair about our sin. We all know what it is like. We pray, we plead with God, 'Keep me from rash words, heated comments, impulsiveness, etc.' But the very next moment we fail. When faced with a particular set of circumstances, we go and do again what we have just renounced. Isn't that enough to make us despair? Then the evil one comes along and tries to convince us, 'This is pointless. You don't have a chance.

You're aiming too high. Be like others and just ignore such things. Enjoy life. Live for now . . .'

Satan is trying to insinuate that we are a hopeless case, but the Lord calls us to resist sin by faith and to cling firmly to the truth of salvation: 'I have been crucified with Christ, so that I may no longer be enslaved to sin.' Jesus' saving act at Calvary is greater than what I can see of His redemption in my life. It is dangerous to consider the mountain of my sin as being greater than Jesus' all-sufficient work of redemption. If I do that, I am holding His sacrifice in contempt and denying His resurrection victory.

Yielding to despair spells our downfall. But one day all doubt and despair will have to give way to the victory of Jesus if I believe in my heart as a certainty that I have actually died to sin and firmly reckon with this fact. Through Christ's death the power of my sinful nature was shattered. So, unswerving in faith, we should time and time again regard ourselves as being dead to sin — even when sin raises its head most brazenly. It is a matter of persevering. In doing so, we glorify the Lamb of God. When we trust Jesus and, despite appearances, firmly take our stand upon the fact that He has put our sin to death, this is a comfort to Him and a proof to Him of our love.

So I can be alive to God in Christ Jesus (6:11). I live in Christ to the extent that I cling to Him in the midst of spiritual darkness and inner conflict. I am far away from Him only when I fail to take sin seriously and to fight it. As soon as I stop pleading for His victory to be manifested, my fellowship with the Lord is disrupted. The person really practising faith is like a little child who, in unfamiliar surroundings, keeps turning to its mother and taking her hand. So the person who believes seeks again and again to humble himself before Jesus. In spirit clinging to the foot of the cross, he looks up into the face of Jesus, claiming His sacrifice and declaring, 'The Bible says that in You I am dead to sin and that Your victory is mine. I am united with You in a death like Yours and share in Your resurrection life.'

God often allows us to be released from our sinful bondage only gradually, a bit at a time. It may even take years, but in the end He does grant release. If we had but an inkling of the suffering Jesus endured as the Lamb of God when He took away our sins and the sins of the whole world, then for His sake we would patiently keep up the struggle against our sins until God grants us deliverance in His good time. In this way we will be given an ever deeper understanding of Jesus' sufferings, through which we receive forgiveness and newness of life.

The more I am aware of my sin, the more I reach out in faith to Jesus and His victory. When a person is in danger, he runs to take cover. When we realize that we are in very real danger because of our sin, we take refuge in Jesus' sacrifice. So our sin serves to bring us the greatest gift: the Lord Himself.

The more God judges us by His Spirit and the more unbearable sin becomes to us, the more we will follow Paul's entreaty, 'Let not sin therefore reign in your mortal bodies, to make you obey their passions' (6:12). However, the more we cling to Christ, the more active Satan will be. We will discover that our sinning does not consist of isolated incidents, like telling a lie. It is a controlling influence. For example, if we are suddenly humiliated, perhaps because we can no longer do a certain job or are replaced by someone more gifted, we become aware of the selfish ambition and pride motivating us. By nature we do not have the attitude of Jesus Christ: He humbled Himself, going so far as actually to die a criminal's death on a cross.

Sin, originating from Satan, is a force that dominates us, driving us like a tree driven by the wind. This is why Paul urges us, 'Let not sin therefore reign in your mortal bodies' (6:12). It is a matter of life and death for us. Either sin rules us, or we gain the victory over it. It is either the rule of Satan or the rule of Jesus Christ.

Sin holds the greatest sway in our lives when we play down its seriousness by rationalizing and defending our actions, insisting we could not help but act the way we did. This can go so far that we excuse ourselves — for example, for having been arrogant and domineering — by saying piously, 'If only you knew how much I have struggled not to be like that!' Perhaps we don't say so aloud, but we are full of self-pity over our failure and persuade ourselves that, after all, we have prayed and struggled. In the end we're always right! Finding excuses, blaming anything and anyone but oneself — this is what Satan has been instigating people to do ever since the Fall.

'Do not yield your members to sin as instruments of wickedness, but yield yourselves to God as men who have been brought from death to life, and your members to God as instruments of righteousness. For sin will have no dominion over you, since you are not under law but under grace' (6:13-14). Once more Paul refers to the rule of sin. He wants to impress on us: It is not a question of specific sins in our lives, but rather a matter of forces trying to control us. So we are called to surrender ourselves to righteousness and grace.

If we are to commit ourselves to His righteousness with all our being, we need to let God judge us and to convict us of sin. We have to be willing to see ourselves for the sinners that we are. As we stand humbled in the presence of God and others, nothing remains of our good opinion of ourselves. But then God draws near to us with His grace, which is our covering. God is waiting for the moment when we surrender ourselves, so that He can grant us grace because of Calvary.

Only in the measure that we submit to God's holiness and accept the rightness of His judgment — even when it comes to us through others — will we realize the depth of His mercy. This way we can be 'instruments of righteousness' (6:13). But we can also be 'instruments of mercy' and rejoice in Christ, because we stand corrected, accepting the truth, as well as being under His grace. Then we experience what it means that He has broken sin's hold on us.

We may think that what the apostle describes in verses 11 to 14 will happen very quickly. But this is not so. It is a long, painful growing process, requiring much patience.

We learn to live by grace only with difficulty — because grace is always preceded by judgment. So we need to pray, 'Give me a real desire to be corrected by others and to take their words to heart as judgment coming from You. Give me the grace to recognize Your judgment in every humiliation, in every failure.' We need to be alert and receptive to God's judgments. Whether He sends His judgment directly, or indirectly through people, it is only when we are under His judgment that we truly grasp the significance of Jesus' sacrifice. Only then will our faith be kindled. Only then will we be filled with the assurance that the Lamb of God has actually put to death the sinful forces exposed by His judgment.

Only to the extent that I am really living in Jesus, and He in me, will I feel grief for my sins. For His sake I cannot accept grace indifferently, taking it for granted. In His overflowing love for us, Jesus paid a high price for His glorious victory at Easter. Now He has attained the purpose of His suffering: we need no longer be slaves of sin, for we are under God's grace (6:14) and can testify to a new life through and in Christ.

6:15-17
What then? Are we to sin because we are not under law but under grace? By no means! Do you not know that if you yield yourselves to any one as obedient slaves, you are slaves of the one whom you obey, either of sin, which leads to death, or of obedience, which leads to righteousness? But thanks be to God, that you who were once slaves of sin have become obedient from the heart to the standard of teaching to which you were committed . . .

Will we be able to handle freedom from the law in the right spirit? Without the law as a prop, won't we go on sinning? No! Grace acts as a safeguard for us if we consciously choose obedience, which leads to righteousness, and if we commit ourselves to obey. Then grace increasingly becomes a power within us and releases us from the slavery to sin, since we are now in Christ.

The Jewish Christians in Rome evidently thought that because they had the law, everything was all right. But having the law, or knowing it, is not what matters. What counts is which master I choose to serve — sin or righteousness? To serve sin spells death, but to obey God leads to righteousness. Which is my real master?

6:18-23

. . . and [you], having been set free from sin, have become slaves of righteousness. I am speaking in human terms, because of your natural limitations. For just as you once yielded your members to impurity and to greater and greater iniquity, so now yield your members to right-eousness for sanctification.

When you were slaves of sin, you were free in regard to righteousness. But then what return did you get from the things of which you are now ashamed? The end of those things is death. But now that you have been set free from sin and have become slaves of God, the return you get is sanctification and its end, eternal life. For the wages of sin is death, but the free gift of God is eternal life in Christ Jesus our Lord.

To be a slave of righteousness means belonging to Jesus Christ. It means being fully surrendered to Him, just as previously I had given myself to sin. Of course we don't *want* to serve sin. Even so, we are unwilling to commit ourselves unreservedly to Jesus and to die to self. We are lulled into a false sense of security by the law, which we know so well but which we cannot keep by our own efforts — a fact we fail to register.

Either we belong to sin, or else we belong to our Lord Jesus Christ. These two extremes are expressed here by the word 'slave'. With that, the mutual exclusiveness of the respective position is made clear (6:19). The apostle speaks this way, using the illustration of slaves and masters, because it is easy to understand. Every day anew we need to decide whether we want to be slaves of righteousness or slaves of sin. How far-reaching are the effects of such a decision! The more we are enslaved by sin, the more we come under the power of death (6:21) — the death of boredom and futility. We are not being fruitful for the Lord.

When we allow Jesus Christ to release us more and more from sin, this — according to Scripture — does not imply that we are sinless. However, sin has lost its mastery over us — in the sense that we are no longer blind to it and that it no longer constantly rules over us. But has sin actually lost its mastery over our lives in this way? Are we in reality slaves of God, which means dedicating ourselves, in love, to serve Him? Only then will we one day receive eternal life (6:23) — that is, be at home in the City of God, whose centre is the victorious Lamb.

ROMANS
—SEVEN—

Are we really living by grace (6:14)? Or is the concept of forgiveness of sin by grace merely an empty formula in our lives? If so, this is a sign that we are less concerned about receiving God's merciful love than about maintaining a show of religion, behind which sin can continue to reign in us. In order to protect us from this deception, which would have dangerous consequences for all eternity, the apostle expounds on the position of the law.

7:1-6
Do you not know, brethren — for I am speaking to those who know the law — that the law is binding on a person only during his life? Thus a married woman is bound by law to her husband as long as he lives; but if her husband dies she is discharged from the law concerning the husband. Accordingly, she will be called an adulteress if she lives with another man while her husband is alive. But if her husband dies she is free from that law, and if she marries another man she is not an adulteress.

Likewise, my brethren, you have died to the law through the body of Christ, so that you may belong to another, to him who has been raised from the dead in order that we may bear fruit for God. While we were liv-

ing in the flesh, our sinful passions, aroused by the law, were at work in our members to bear fruit for death. But now we are discharged from the law, dead to that which held us captive, so that we serve not under the old written code but in the new life of the Spirit.

Paul gives an example from Jewish theocratic life. Through marriage, which was indissoluble by law, the wife is bound to her husband (7:2). So the wife cannot leave her husband, even if she wanted to. However, the law has no power to kindle in the woman love for her husband. The distressing state of a loveless marriage remains until the husband dies. But then the law no longer has any right to condemn the woman if she wants to marry another man.

The apostle uses this as an illustration for our spiritual life as Christians. For us, too, it is important that the law can find no reason to accuse us of violating its holy claims. Yet the law has precisely the effect of provoking the sin dwelling in us (7:5). 'The sting of death is sin, and the power of sin is the law' (1 Corinthians 15:56). In other words, the law reveals our sins. The law awakens opposition in our hearts and so defeats its own purpose. If I tell a child, 'Do this', he'll reply, 'No!' But if I say to him, 'Here is something special for you to do — a real privilege for you', then he is suddenly willing.

Even though God's overflowing love comes to us in His holy will, our sinful nature reacts against it. We reject His will and are disobedient as soon as His will comes to us as a law or obligation.

Why is this so? The law requires us to give up something we don't want to give up. We want to have the last word and cling to our rights. We want to assert ourselves and see our demands fulfilled. We want to defend ourselves instead of remaining silent. We want to receive rather than give. We want to criticize rather than be merciful. So when the law requires of us something we don't want, it has the effect of making our sinful nature assert itself all the more. Aroused by the law, we produce fruit for death (7:5b) and remain under the old written code (7:6b).

Now comes the great turning-point: 'But if her husband dies . . .' (7:2). Because he is dead, the woman is released. She is free to marry another man, for the law has no more claims on her. If the woman had selflessly won her husband over by her love, she would not have wanted to leave him. However, she was not selfless, and so the law had to watch over her and condemn her if she committed a self-willed action.

The law is, in fact, good and shows us what God requires of us. However, because of our sinful nature it cannot help us to do what God expects of us: to love where by nature we do not love.

Paul considers this analogy of a wife and her husband significant for our relationship to our Lord Jesus Christ. How different is our relationship to Him from our relationship to the law! Our

Redeemer does not demand that we fulfil the law by overcoming our sins, for we are unable to do so. He has freed us from the dominion of sin. 'My brethren, you have died to the law through the body of Christ' (7:4a). Because of Jesus' death, we have nothing more to do with the law in the sense of being obliged to fulfil it in our own strength. We are not left to our fate. Self-effort puts us at the mercy of the law and, in effect, asserts the rule of sin over us. Instead, we are released from the law, having 'died to the law through the body of Christ'.

Therefore, we can never praise God enough for the mystery of Christ's incarnation. By assuming a human body, Jesus could bear the punishment in our stead as both man and God. A legal transaction has taken place. When the body of Jesus Christ was put to death, our sin, which He took upon Himself in that body, was also put to death.

This stirring, joyous message has been vividly depicted by the great fifteenth-century artist Matthias Grünewald in a work of art now in the National Gallery of Art, in Washington, D.C. In this painting of the crucifixion, the body of Christ is visibly covered with our sin. The wounds in His right knee resemble the horns of an animal, and above the chest cavity two human eyes peer at us disapprovingly. All this is intended to express the fact that our sin was put to death with Christ.

Through Jesus, in His crucified body, our sin is put to death. Consequently, we are also dead to the law, which condemns our sin. The law has no more power over us. If our sin has died with the body of Christ, then the law has nothing more to condemn in us. We are in the same position as the wife when her husband has died. The law binding her to her husband is no longer in force. It cannot forbid her to take another husband.

Because of our identification with the body of Christ, crucified for our sins, we are free from sin's control and from the law's demands. The law can no longer accuse us. Our jealousy, selfish ambition, obstinacy, fault-finding, and sinful cravings were put to death in His body. Hence the jubilant cry, ' . . . so that you may belong to another' — namely, Jesus, the Prince of Victory, 'who has been raised from the dead' (7:4).

Now it is up to us to accept this gracious gift of His love. If we do so, we will become increasingly aware that there is in fact nothing good to be found in us.

Some years ago I prayed earnestly to the Lord that He might humble me because of a certain sin, for I noticed that all my prayers to be released from it were of no avail. I remained hardened and unchanged on this point. Then it happened that I grieved someone very much by this behaviour of mine — and on a special occasion at that. I cried to the Lord, 'I can't go on the way I am. My life must show that I belong to another, to Him who was raised from the dead. Give me tears over my sin. Let Your grace have dominion over me.' I wrote this down and asked the Lord — and this was very hard for me — to humble me in front of others as well.

Months later He fulfilled my request. God placed me in His searchlight as never before. His holiness seemed to consume me. But then, as I happened to be leafing through my diary containing my personal notes and prayers, the Holy Spirit led me to this very prayer! I could only thank the Lord and say, 'You are dealing with me in order to free me from a life under the law and under the rule of sin, by making me so painfully aware of my sin. You want to make me entirely Yours.'

Yes, we have the privilege of belonging 'to another, to him who has been raised from the dead in order that we may bear fruit for God' (7:4) — genuine fruit, which only Christ can produce in us. Not by our own effort and deeds, but by the deep fellowship of love with Him are we able to bear fruit — fruit of which we know nothing. According to Matthew 25, the righteous will ask the Lord in amazement when they fed and clothed Him.

Our Lord, crucified for us, gave His all that we might 'serve . . . in the new life of the Spirit' (7:6), and to this end He continually works in us through His Holy Spirit. God forces nobody but waits for our commitment. This will help us to accept His dealings. When we come under His chastening and judgment, we also come under His grace. What a blessing 'to belong to another'! It is very wonderful to live by His power a life to His glory as wretched sinners, instead of struggling to fulfil the law by ourselves, clinging to our own righteousness, which is accursed in the sight of God.

If we 'belong to another', then we notice when Jesus looks at us and says, 'Now's the moment to give a bold testimony' or, 'Now's the moment to be silent.' At first we won't be so aware of this. But as we pray to Jesus and converse with Him in love, He will draw closer and closer to us. As we yearn with all our hearts to be released from our self-centred, legalistic nature and have but one thought, 'If I have You, Lord Jesus, I have all I need!', He will gain more and more room in our lives.

Then I will begin to weep over my sins with genuine grief. This is not admitting the wrongness of my actions merely with the intellect — 'I should not have done that. I'm sorry.' It is Jesus Christ now enlightening me by His Spirit so that, like Peter, I can weep over what I'm doing to Jesus by my sins. Jesus' eyes see deeper than the law, which judges our actions only on the outside. By His life-giving Spirit, Jesus approaches from within. He shows me my guilt and how much it grieves Him when I am so sure of myself in my opinions about others. By renewing us inwardly, His Spirit makes 'Christ in us' more and more of a reality. Now the law has to address its claims to Christ, who both satisfies the demands of the law and fulfils them in my life. His Spirit constrains me to do His will in love and with joy, 'that we may bear fruit for God' (7:4).

7:7-13

What then shall we say? That the law is sin? By no means! Yet, if it had not been for the law, I should not have known sin. I should not have known what it is to covet if the law had not said, 'You shall not covet.' But sin, finding opportunity in the commandment, wrought in me all kinds of covetousness. Apart from the law sin lies dead. I was once alive apart from the law, but when the commandment came, sin revived and I died; the very commandment which promised life proved to be death to me. For sin, finding opportunity in the commandment, deceived me and by it killed me. So the law is holy, and the commandment is holy and just and good.

Did that which is good, then, bring death to me? By no means! It was sin, working death in me through what is good, in order that sin might be shown to be sin, and through the commandment might become sinful beyond measure.

From his own life the apostle shares how he came to receive a faith that brings release from the law of sin and death. It started before his encounter with Jesus Christ. 'I should not have known what it is to covet if the law had not said, "You shall not covet"' (7:7). So without having met the Saviour, Paul recognized how terrible sin is. The demands of the law (7:9) arouse opposition in us, provoking us to do the very thing we ought not to do. It stimulates the sin that is alive within us. This was Paul's experience when he came up against the 'You shall not'. At first, God's commandment did not affect him personally; but when it began to make real demands on his daily life, 'sin revived' (7:9). The desire to sin was stimulated, coming into conflict with the commandment of the holy God.

So sin is activated precisely when the holy law of God is meant to set us on the right track. This is the natural relationship between God in His holiness and fallen man, who has been expelled from paradise. 'I died; the very commandment which promised life proved to be death to me' (7:9-10).

Such experiences are familiar to us all. We have heard, for instance, God's commandment to break with our self-will or to keep ourselves pure in body, soul and spirit. When we really take this to heart, we begin to resist sin, only to discover how weak we are. Someone else is on the scene — Satan! He now starts an offensive so vigorous that we grow weary. All we can see is our continual failure. Consequently, we are tempted to give up the struggle, an attitude Paul summed up in the words 'I died'. Paraphrased, this means: 'I have become immune to the commandment of God. I knew it but couldn't fulfil it. So I turned a deaf ear to it. That which should really have helped me to find new life simply brought death. Now I was completely separated from God.'

This shows that without Christ the law has the effect of sentencing us to death. If we live without Christ — that is, in our own strength — we don't have the light, which helps us to see ourselves as wretched sinners and to come to repentance. If we did, our constant cry would be, 'Where can I take refuge? Only in You, Lord Jesus!'

7:14-25
We know that the law is spiritual; but I am carnal, sold under sin. I do not understand my own actions. For I do not do what I want, but I do the very thing I hate. Now if I do what I do not want, I agree that the law is good. So then it is no longer I that do it, but sin which dwells within me. For I know that nothing good dwells within me, that is, in my flesh. I can will what is right, but I cannot do it. For I do not do the good I want, but the evil I do not want is what I do. Now if I do what I do not want, it is no longer I that do it, but sin which dwells within me.

So I find it to be a law that when I want to do right, evil lies close at hand. For I delight in the law of God, in my inmost self, but I see in my members another law at war with the law of my mind and making me captive to the law of sin which dwells in my members. Wretched man that I am! Who will deliver me from this body of death? Thanks be to God through Jesus Christ our Lord! So then, I of myself serve the law of God with my mind, but with my flesh I serve the law of sin.

Paul had been referring to his former life, but now he switches to the present tense. He speaks of the new life that began for him on the road to Damascus, when the bright light of Jesus overwhelmed him. Now the apostle becomes aware of God's demands. Now he is distressed by his sin. 'I do not understand my own actions. For I do not do what I want, but I do the very thing I hate' (7:15). 'Nothing good dwells within me, that is, in my flesh. I can will what is right, but I cannot do it' (7:18).

This statement reflects Paul's personal experience. When Jesus in His holiness encountered Paul and when His light penetrated the depths of Paul's heart, then he saw his sin and at the same time recognized Jesus as his Saviour, who had borne all his sins. But his understanding of Jesus' saving act was not to remain a one-time experience, nor to degenerate into mere words, a matter of the intellect. Rather there was to be a continuous outworking of this saving act in his life.

The same applies to us. Faith in Jesus Christ, faith in His taking away our sin, entails a struggle — a process lasting from my first encounter with Jesus Christ to my dying breath. The ultimate goal is that He will rule over every area of my life. But this I have to grasp in faith, for it is not something I will see in this life.

This is the tension, the conflict, in which the apostle finds himself (7:14-25). Facing reality, he exclaims, 'Wretched man that I am! Who will deliver me from this body of death?' (7:24). Because on earth we are still living in the body, Satan will always be finding ways to attack us and to break into our life. As long as I am in the flesh, the prince of this world has access to me; in this life I will always be susceptible to temptation — even if I am born again through faith in Jesus Christ. The attacks of the devil are only overcome by continually trusting in our Redeemer, and never through an apathetic, passive attitude that says, 'Victory will come automatically.' No, we are involved in a battle.

'I can will what is right, but I cannot do it . . . Who will deliver me from this body of death?' (7:18, 24). Here Paul is saying, 'I am still a mortal man. My conversion was not the end but the beginning of a spiritual development, through the work of the Holy Spirit.' When I realize that 'nothing good dwells within me' (7:18), I need to take up the battle of faith and resist sin. The old nature under the rule of Satan fights against the new nature under the Lordship of Jesus Christ. Yet this conflict between seeing myself as a wretched sinner and at the same time laying hold of what Jesus won for me — this is what keeps me in Him.

When this tension is not sustained in reality, we are living in hypocrisy. Like Paul, we must constantly take care that we are maintaining the struggle between the flesh and the spirit in holy fear that we don't miss the heavenly goal.

It is a matter of seeing ourselves for what we are — 'Wretched man that I am!' — and countering this realization with the triumphant declaration: 'Thanks be to God through Jesus Christ our Lord, who has redeemed me!' With all his might the enemy tries to drag us back into our old life. Through our corruptible body, our sinful nature, the devil still has access to us. This calls for a constant battle of faith. Otherwise we will forfeit the glory at the throne of God — the glory Jesus won for us by His death.

If we keep up the battle of faith, we will find that the condition of being a wretched sinner, sad and painful as it may seem, will fill us with a secret joy. Then we are in the right frame to meet Jesus afresh. The light of truth, which convicts us of sin, always leads us to the place of refuge: Jesus Christ.

ROMANS
— EIGHT —

8:1-4

There is therefore now no condemnation for those who are in Christ Jesus. For the law of the Spirit of life in Christ Jesus has set me free from the law of sin and death. For God has done what the law, weakened by the flesh, could not do: sending his own Son in the likeness of sinful flesh and for sin, he condemned sin in the flesh, in order that the just requirement of the law might be fulfilled in us, who walk not according to the flesh but according to the Spirit.

Christ does not condemn any sinner who admits his sin and clings to Him in faith. Although we are created in the image of God, our fallen human nature remains sin-tainted to the end. Yet there is no condemnation awaiting those who live in union with Jesus Christ, because Jesus has taken upon Himself the sentence we deserve. If I am 'in Christ Jesus' — that is, if I again and again seek refuge in Him on account of my sins — then Jesus increasingly releases me from my sinful nature and causes His Spirit to rule in me.

In so far as I actually live 'in Christ Jesus', I will experience newness of life. The power of the Spirit will make me spiritually alive and enable me to see sin for what it is. No longer can I be accused on account of my sin. The verdict I deserve has fallen upon Jesus Christ, in whom 'I stow myself away', as Luther put it.

God sent His only Son in a physical body like ours, so as to put our sin to death in His body. Jesus paid the penalty for our sin. The power of sin was broken, and His Spirit can bring about in us the obedience and love that God seeks in us, His children.

This does not mean, however, that the Spirit automatically prompts me to act as God wishes me to, so that I perfectly fulfil His commandments: loving Him above all else and my neighbour as myself. We may come across this misconception in Christian circles. Some claim that baptism in the Spirit means the end of all sinning, while others say being born again means that our sin-loving nature has disappeared for good.

The statement 'There is therefore now no condemnation for those who are in Christ Jesus' (8:1) is uttered by Paul in a spirit of triumphant faith. It does not express a static condition. To my dying breath I remain prone to sin. But through God's intervention, through Jesus' saving act, I receive His Spirit, who convicts me and at the same time gives me the grace of contrition, repentance and love for Jesus.

We live in a state of tension. Being in the flesh, we are still vulnerable to Satan's temptations. But if we turn to our Lord Jesus Christ in steadfast faith, we will experience the power of His redemption progressively freeing us from sin. This will be combined with an ever deeper disappointment in ourselves, enabling us to grasp all the more clearly that 'God has done what the law . . . could not do: sending his own Son' (8:3). God does not condemn us for our sin. Rather, He came to us in Jesus to condemn our sin in His body and to put it to death.

Even so, the assurance of salvation can degenerate into self-complacency. Satan will do anything to lull us into a false sense of security. For instance, he uses an over-emphasis on charismatic gifts or the teaching of cheap grace: 'All I have to do is believe in Jesus, and I'll go to heaven.' The danger here lies in the misconception that for us Christians there is no longer any imperative, no commandment of God to obey, only a state of being: 'I am saved. I've consciously received the Holy Spirit. And now I am living a "new life" and will one day enter into the heavenly glory.'

Certainly, righteousness in Christ is fulfilled in us as we live according to the Spirit. This is the jubilant cry of verse 4. But because it is 'costly grace', our experience continues to be in the present tense: 'I can will what is right, but I cannot do it . . . Wretched man that I am!' (7:18, 24). Who has not painfully had to admit this again and again? How often the Lord has had to confront us with what we are like! For instance, we may have disappointed others, showing that, despite appearances, we are not trustworthy.

Nevertheless, Jesus by His death on the cross has won for us the life-giving Spirit, who leads us more and more into new life in and with Christ.

Mary of Egypt, a well-known figure in Early Christian times, was a living testimony to the creative power of the Spirit when He enters a person's life as the Spirit of truth and of repentance. As a young girl, she is said to have run away from home and ended up in the seaport of Alexandria, where she fell into bad ways. For love of adventure she boarded a ship on which was a group of pilgrims headed for Jerusalem. Out of curiosity Mary decided to visit the Church of the Holy Sepulchre with them. But when she tried to follow them into this holy place commemorating the death and resurrection of Jesus, the Holy Spirit met her and she was stopped in her tracks.

Quick as a flash of lightning, Mary saw that her sinful life was the barrier. It was as if she had seen Jesus, her Saviour, looking at her. In deep sorrow she wept over her sins and experienced renewal from within. A new life began for her in Jesus. As she received more and more light about her sinful nature, she was gripped with a growing love for Him. The desire henceforth to live a life of prayer and worship caused her to withdraw into the solitude of the desert.

This new life in Christ Jesus frees us from the old vicious circle of sin and death; but, as has been said, this is a life-long process. So Paul writes to the Ephesians that we are to grow up into Christ (Ephesians 4:15). For this reason he removes from the fellowship those who, although they began well, continue to sin deliberately, without repenting (1 Corinthians 5:1-5). So we need to fight the battle of faith daily. Certainly, Christ has redeemed us from the condemnation brought upon us by our sin (8:1). We are no longer under compulsion to obey the dictates of the flesh, in spiritual blindness. Rather, we now live according to the prompting of the Spirit. But following after the Holy Spirit means living in the light. In the light nothing alive remains as it is: it is transformed. So living in His light, living in obedience to the promptings of the Spirit, implies change. Our life takes a new direction: we follow Jesus step by step on His path and allow Him to fill us increasingly with His righteousness.

When Mary of Egypt knew she was called to the solitude of the desert to spend her life in contrition and repentance, this was a sign that the light of the Holy Spirit had really struck her and that her experience was genuine. If we ask Him, the Lord will clearly show us how we, too, can demonstrate a change of heart. For each of us it will be something different. But one aspect will be the same. The more the Lord sanctifies us through His precious blood, the more we will weep over our sin. And the more tears we shed, the more we will commit ourselves to do the exact opposite of what we used to do.

This might mean, for instance, making a clean break with someone — if my thoughts or emotions focus too much on that person. Or it may mean writing a letter admitting a falsehood. It means praying to the Lord that His life-giving Spirit might gain room in me, enabling me to say, 'I don't want to have anything more to do with this sin! The old has passed away.' Such an attitude shows that I am responding to the Spirit's admonition. Then the words will increasingly become a reality in my life: 'The law of the Spirit of life in Christ Jesus has set me free from the law of sin and death' (8:2).

It is sad but true that we may know God's Word in Romans 3 to 5 practically by heart and yet fail to wage a real battle of faith against sin and to mend our ways. We are playing straight into the hands of Satan, who wants to sift us like wheat (Luke 22:31) and claim victims even among the disciples of Jesus. But when Jesus sees we are ready to show by our actions that we are sorry, He hastens to us and fills us more and more with His life-giving Spirit. This in turn will enable us to better recognize sin for what it is, and by the power of His holy sacrifice we will conceive a greater hatred of sin. Even if it is a long process, we will increasingly experience release from sin.

Towards the end of World War II, I suddenly noticed that my thoughts were unduly taken up with the mother of one of the girls who came to our Bible classes, and that the pleasure of talking with her was keeping me from prayer. It was at a time when I was no longer faithfully fighting my battle of faith, and accordingly my first love for Jesus had faded. Then God in His love showed me: You are on the wrong track; turn around.

After that, I stopped seeing her. One evening the daughter of this woman came to me for counselling. Suddenly, the sirens went off. We realized it could be a dangerous air raid. There was nothing to do but take the girl home, since it was pitch black outside on the streets. When we were right in front of her parents' house, we could already see the many illumination flares in the sky — the danger signal for an air raid. I was now faced with a decision. Should I take cover in their air-raid shelter, where I would meet the girl's mother, whom I had been avoiding? Or should I turn back? I hesitated for a moment, but then ran back. And immediately afterwards came the dreadful destruction of our city.

The next morning one of the Bible class girls came to see if I was all right. Almost her first sentence was, 'Do you know that Mrs. X (the mother of the girl I had escorted home the previous night) was killed last night?' This very house, including its air-raid shelter, had been hit by a heavy bomb. If I had gone into the shelter in disobedience to God, I would have died that night. This was a lesson to me how seriously God's commands are to be taken.

'What the law could not do [that is, break the power of sin in us] . . . God did by sending His own Son in the likeness of sinful flesh' (8:3 RAV). Jesus' sacrifice was an act of inexpressible love, and so for His sake we should abhor sin. Because Jesus Christ allowed Himself to be condemned on the cross in order that we might not be eternally damned, we must learn to hate sin. This means walking not 'according to the flesh', permitting ourselves anything and everything, but walking 'according to the Spirit'. This is not to say that we will not sin, for we will do so till the day we die. However, if we walk 'according to the Spirit', we will be filled with sorrow over every time we have sinned and failed again. We will take the next step of obedience that His Spirit shows us.

For Jesus it is always a triumph when we weep over our sin. Then He no longer takes any notice of it, seeing only our tears and rejoicing over them. What a wonderful Lord! We tend to think that when our pride and self-righteousness are shattered, all we can do is despair. But the opposite is true. Those who humble themselves will be exalted. Though I have often found it hard to humble myself in front of others, whenever I did so, Christ drew closer to me. When our Lord Jesus Christ gives us His light of truth, it is not all pain. Rather, we will experience deep joy in Him. The truth in Christ may well separate us from some, but it also grants us the true fellowship of love with God and with one another, as together we walk 'according to the Spirit'. This is the meaning of the jubilant song of victory in the first verses of Romans 8.

8:5-11

For those who live according to the flesh set their minds on the things of the flesh, but those who live according to the Spirit, the things of the Spirit. For to be carnally minded is death, but to be spiritually minded is life and peace. Because the carnal mind is enmity against God; for it is not subject to the law of God, nor indeed can be. So then, those who are in the flesh cannot please God. But you are not in the flesh but in the Spirit, if indeed the Spirit of God dwells in you. Now if anyone does not have the Spirit of Christ, he is not His. And if Christ is in you, the body is dead because of sin, but the Spirit is life because of righteousness. But if the Spirit of Him who raised Jesus from the dead dwells in you, He who raised Christ from the dead will also give life to your mortal bodies through His Spirit who dwells in you.
(RAV)

It is precisely my weakness and powerlessness which challenges me to have faith. And by believing and trusting Him, I demonstrate my love for Him. Sinless perfection is not the issue. What Jesus looks for in us is faith — faith when we can't see. Such faith is the expression of the greatest love, which He seeks in us, because He is love.

When this love has no place in me, then I am carnally minded — that is, dead. Just as oxygen is essential to physical life, so is the Spirit of light and truth essential to a life of spiritual love. Without His Spirit I am spiritually dead. Spiritual death, however, means enmity towards God (8:7). This carnal attitude begins with even the smallest transgression of God's commandments. The more I tolerate the transgression, the more indifferent I become towards God, His Word and will.

If God's Spirit dwells in us, we are not apathetic towards our sin. Even though we may fall into sin many times in a single day, we do not gloss over it but are grieved. Through the resurrection life of Jesus, we become spiritually minded, and divine life is in us. We become sensitive to sin and sensitive to Jesus Himself. We will have a growing awareness of His suffering at Calvary as well as of His present-day sufferings through the falling away of so many, even within the Christian Church.

Being spiritually minded means having peace with God through Christ in our inmost hearts. Nor is that all. If the Spirit of God lives in us, we have the guarantee that we will not be at the mercy of the Prince of Death. Rather, we will be raised up to be with our Lord Jesus Christ for ever.

Paul was very concerned that the church in Rome should be able to recognize the mutually exclusive forces of 'the Spirit of God' and 'flesh' operating in our lives. For this reason he writes so explicitly that the Spirit of Christ must dwell in us. The Spirit gives us life, so that when we decide to surrender ourselves to God in obedience, our decision results in action: we take the next step. Only when both the will and action are present, is Christ in us. Willingness on its own is not sufficient. Evidence of complete yieldedness should follow, demonstrating that Christ is living in us (8:10).

8:12-16
So then, brethren, we are debtors, not to the flesh, to live according to the flesh — for if you live according to the flesh you will die, but if by the Spirit you put to death the deeds of the body you will live. For all who are led by the Spirit of God are sons of God. For you did not receive the spirit of slavery to fall back into fear, but you have received the spirit of sonship. When we cry, 'Abba! Father!' it is the Spirit himself bearing witness with our spirit that we are children of God . . .

If by the Spirit we are to put to death the deeds — or rather, misdeeds — of the body, then fighting the good fight should be an urgent priority in our lives. The deeds of the body can be summed up as self-centredness, which makes us apathetic towards sin. This is a call to keep up the struggle, so that the Spirit really does gain more and more room in our lives. The fruit of such a battle is that 'you will live' (8:13). True life in and for God means doing His will. This is the evidence of being a real child of God. And we show that we are His children when we feel compelled to admit the truth, to walk in the light, to do His will. Doing God's will wholeheartedly always results in peace with God as a gift of the Holy Spirit. When the Spirit lives in us, we have complete freedom and yet are prompted by Him to do God's will, even when it goes against our reason and old nature.

'All who are led by the Spirit of God are sons of God.' To have 'the spirit of sonship' means that my deepest longing is to do God's will, the will of the Father. To choose to be dependent upon Him is the ultimate freedom of a child of God. The Holy Spirit confirms my sonship. This guards me against the wrong kind of fear. Satan tries to separate me from the Father. But in all my trials and temptations, I may approach the Father in complete assurance, trusting Him to help me (8:15). It is through my Lord Jesus Christ that I have become a child of the Father. So as a child I may cry, 'Abba, Father!' A trusting attitude will make all rebellious thoughts fade away.

Again and again the Spirit of God affirms (8:16) how greatly God loves me and that I really am His child and can rejoice in this. He constantly reminds me that I am a child of the Father. When He gives me tears over my sin, He also prompts me to cry out, full of trust, 'Abba, dear Father!'

8:17-18
. . . and if children, then heirs, heirs of God and fellow heirs with Christ, provided we suffer with him in order that we may also be glorified with him. I consider that the sufferings of this present time are not worth comparing with the glory that is to be revealed to us.

As His children we are heirs of God and fellow heirs with Christ, the true heir. We are to share in the heavenly inheritance. Jesus' prayer is to be answered: 'Father, I desire that they also, whom thou hast given me, may be with me where I am, to behold my glory . . .' (John 17:24). The glory which we are called to partake of in heaven is holiness. In this state we will be free from self and totally immersed in God, honouring and worshipping Him together with all the angels and overcomers (Revelation 4 and 5).

We receive this glory only to the extent that we suffer with Christ here on earth (8:17). On paths of suffering He frees us from earthly things and from self. He chastens and refines us because of our sins, so that we may become pure and transparent. That is why these sufferings are not worth comparing with the glory He will give us later (8:18).

The more willing we are to be purified by suffering during our lifetime, the nearer Jesus is to us in His love, and the more He will awaken in us the longing to see Him in heaven, where we are to share in His glory. The years of suffering on earth are limited, but the glory that awaits us above lasts for ever. We are willing to stake much on human goals. Ought we not to be far more willing to suffer and to give all we have for the sake of the heavenly glory?

8:19-27

For the creation waits with eager longing for the revealing of the sons of God; for the creation was subjected to futility, not of its own will but by the will of him who subjected it in hope; because the creation itself will be set free from its bondage to decay and obtain the glorious liberty of the children of God. We know that the whole creation has been groaning in travail together until now; and not only the creation, but we ourselves, who have the first fruits of the Spirit, groan inwardly as we wait for adoption as sons, the redemption of our bodies. For in this hope we were saved. Now hope that is seen is not hope. For who hopes for what he sees? But if we hope for what we do not see, we wait for it with patience.

Likewise the Spirit helps us in our weakness; for we do not know how to pray as we ought, but the Spirit himself intercedes for us with sighs too deep for words. And he who searches the hearts of men knows what is the mind of the Spirit, because the Spirit intercedes for the saints according to the will of God.

The goal of human history is the revealing of the sons of God in all their glory. The world is heading for this goal; creation yearns for it (8:19-22); the sons of God themselves long for it. And it is the Holy Spirit who helps us in our weakness to keep our eyes on this goal (8:26-27).

The 'eager longing' of creation (8:19) signifies that the whole natural world is waiting for the moment when God's sons are to be revealed in the full glory of redemption — that is, when those who love the Lord, having been sanctified by suffering, will enter their glorified state. The whole creation still has to wait and suffer, because it is subjected to futility and decay — though not of its own accord, but on account of man's sin (Genesis 3:17-18). Thus creation longs for redemption. Yet it has been given hope. As creation was degraded by man, so it will also be exalted together with redeemed man.

But it is not only creation which longs for the future glory. So do the children of God. It is worth noting that, unlike creation, they yearn for it consciously. When Paul speaks of the longing of God's children for redemption (8:23), he describes them as having the Holy Spirit within them as a foretaste of the future glory. They are filled by the Holy Spirit in body, soul and spirit. When God created man, spirit and body were intended to be a unity, and so the redeemed spirit longs for a redeemed body, free from sinful impulses.

'For in this hope we were saved' (8:24). The emphasis lies on hope, on something we do not yet see, on something which has not yet fully come. In this world the Lordship of Jesus Christ is still limited. Otherwise death would have been abolished altogether. Hope and longing are signs of spiritual life. We need to wait patiently and to press on towards the glorious goal which lies before us: we are heirs of the future glory. Our unredeemed bodies (8:23) actually make us keep straining to reach this goal. As we painfully realize that the sinful desires of the flesh are trying to bind us to this earth, the longing grows all the stronger in us to go straight for the goal, for heaven above, and to live there one day, where our worthless bodies will be gloriously transformed. This is an ongoing struggle requiring patience.

False emotional attachments, and antipathies aroused by the ways and mannerisms of others, are also part of the unredeemed nature of man. The more I suffer because of my sins, and the more my utter helplessness comes to light, the more Jesus draws near to me in His redeeming power. The more this happens, the more I will long to be completely transformed and to attain the future glory.

'The Spirit helps us in our weakness' (8:26). He helps us, weak as we are, not to waver or give up the struggle, till we reach the point of resting completely in God. But it hurts Him when we neglect prayer. He is grieved when in our life of faith we are defeated because we are lukewarm in prayer and don't resist sin.

What a blessing it is that the Holy Spirit fills our spirit, searching our inmost being, detecting and revealing our sins! 'The Spirit himself intercedes for us' (8:26). He does not make us better than what we are; but, when we are weak and in spiritual darkness, He makes intercession on our behalf before God the Father as our Advocate. That which we are often incapable of doing in such situations, He is able to achieve — that is, to pray and come to God. Because of our weakness and inner distress, He pleads for us with 'sighs too deep for words'. It is a great comfort to know that the One who sees into the very depths of our hearts is pleading for us in harmony with God's own will.

8:28-30
We know that in everything God works for good with those who love him, who are called according to his purpose. For those whom he foreknew he also predestined to be conformed to the image of his Son, in order that he might be the first-born among many brethren. And those whom he predestined he also called; and those whom he called he also justified; and those whom he justified he also glorified.

God sends us help not only by His Spirit but also in everything that happens to us (8:28). This doesn't necessarily mean that the circumstances are altered; rather we are given the right direction for every situation in life. We are not speaking here of predestination in the negative sense that some are not called. The emphasis is on the love of God calling us to Himself according to His purpose (8:28). So everything that happens is for the ultimate good of His children. The Spirit is leading them on to the goal of spiritual maturity. This is established in verses 29 and 30. Everything that happens to us is part of the divine plan to conform us to the image of Christ, so that we will be raised with Him to glory and receive the everlasting inheritance.

Why doesn't it say 'conformed to the image of God'? God cannot be seen. But the image of Jesus

Christ is clearly depicted for us. All the features are there for us to see. He has presented His portrait to us in His life: The Lamb of God, who trod the path of obedience, lowliness, forbearance and poverty. The great High Priest ever pleading on our behalf. The Son, whose heart's desire was to be in His Father's house (Luke 2:49). To be transformed into this image is the noble calling of God's children.

In His great love God turns everything to our good. We often think that His will is ruining our lives. But in everything He is drawing us powerfully towards our destiny as heirs of eternal glory. When we grasp this in faith, suffering makes us patient; inner conflict teaches us to trust; temptation serves to strengthen our obedience.

To put it briefly, everything is designed to help prepare us for our eternal inheritance. We are destined to share in all that is Christ's, for God ordained that Jesus would be 'the first-born among many brethren' (8:29). He is the Living One, the Victor over death. So as His brethren we, too, are to overcome death and be raised to life. With unshakeable faith we can trust in this loving plan of God for us when, in the coming time of testing, we may be faced with persecution and great suffering, which the end-time judgments will bring upon the earth.

'Those whom he predestined he also called [through the gospel]; and those whom he called he also justified [through the cross]; and those whom he justified he also glorified [that is, brought them to glory]' (8:30). He shares with us His glory of being one with the Father (John 17:21).

8:31-39

What then shall we say to this? If God is for us, who is against us? He who did not spare his own Son but gave him up for us all, will he not also give us all things with him? Who shall bring any charge against God's elect? It is God who justifies; who is to condemn? Is it Christ Jesus, who died, yes, who was raised from the dead, who is at the right hand of God, who indeed intercedes for us? Who shall separate us from the love of Christ? Shall tribulation, or distress, or persecution, or famine, or nakedness, or peril, or sword? As it is written, 'For thy sake we are being killed all the day long; we are regarded as sheep to be slaughtered.' No, in all these things we are more than conquerors through him who loved us. For I am sure that neither death, nor life, nor angels, nor principalities, nor things present, nor things to come, nor powers, nor height, nor depth, nor anything else in all creation, will be able to separate us from the love of God in Christ Jesus our Lord.

In Romans 8:1-30 marvels have been displayed for us like a string of pearls: God has destroyed sin's control over us; since we are His children, we are fellow heirs with Christ; all that happens to us is working for our good that we may attain our glorious destiny. Now, with all this in mind, Paul concludes: If God is on our side, who or what could ultimately harm us? Not hostile forces. Nor arrogance and divisions among believers. Nor Satan, who accuses God's elect and tries to bring about their downfall. Nor powers that seek to condemn us. Nor outright persecution and suffering. Yet, when trouble strikes, how easily we lose sight of the goal. We are afraid of suffering and unwilling to die to self and to make sacrifices.

In the times in which we are living, it is so important that the mercy we have received from God produces in us the willingness to suffer. Indeed, many are already suffering for His name's sake, and for the rest of us it is no longer a remote possibility. The words 'we are regarded as sheep to be slaughtered' will become increasingly true for all who are His. As weak and sinful beings, we are incapable of remaining faithful to the Lord in our own strength. So what a triumph it is to be able to rejoice in faith that 'in all these things we are more than conquerors through him who loved us'— as our persecuted brothers and sisters testify so movingly!

Adversities of a human or supernatural origin may be ranged against us. Yet nothing can destroy the certainty that God's love and power are greater still, for God delivered His Son up for us and gave us all things with Him. In Him, we receive grace without limit; for Christ, who died and rose again, blots out all our sins and guilt. He will transform us into His image, the image of the Lamb; and so we will be able to win the victory by patient suffering. There is nothing that can separate us from His love. And when we are suffering, He will demon-strate His love most gloriously. He longs for us to receive the grace to overcome in suffering, so that we may attain the goal of eternal glory.

ROMANS

—TWELVE:1–2—

12:1-2

*I beseech you therefore, brethren, by the mercies of God,
that you present your bodies a living sacrifice, holy,
acceptable to God, which is your reasonable service. And
do not be conformed to this world, but be transformed by
the renewing of your mind, that you may prove what is
that good and acceptable and perfect will of God.* (RAV)

We may feel so comfortable with the 'sweet gospel'
of Romans 3 to 8 that we have difficulty relating to
the challenges and warnings of Romans 12
onwards. They seem too restrictive and impossible
to fulfil. Paul with his insight into human nature is
well aware of this. We may know all about justification by grace through faith but regard it merely as
a doctrine — and so fail to apply it to everyday life.
This clash between theory and practice is often a
very real problem. We are familiar with the doctrine
of justification by grace through faith and can talk
knowledgeably about it, but the glory of this message is poorly reflected in our lives.

Fearing that doctrine and life are not in harmony,
Paul writes, 'I beseech you therefore, brethren . . .'
(12:1 RAV). But he cannot continue his exhortation

without adding 'by the mercies of God'. This gives us a quick review of the mercies of God shining forth in chapters 3 to 8, as well as chapters 9 to 11. On the basis of God's mercy revealed in Jesus Christ, Paul can now make his appeal. But first we need to make sure that our experience of God's mercy is genuine. If we have really grasped the miracle of God's mercy in the forgiveness of sin, we cannot fail to respond with love and dedication.

Paul counts on this response. This is why he adds the warnings and challenges of Romans 12 onwards. However, he does not present them as a *demand* of the law. If we have experienced the mercy of God in our lives, our natural reaction will be to obey these admonitions. If divine mercy governs us, we will naturally offer ourselves — literally, our bodies — as a living sacrifice to God. This is where the joyful compulsion expressed in Romans 6:16-18 comes into play. Out of gratitude to Jesus for His forgiveness, we feel we simply must become 'slaves of obedience'. The mercy of Jesus Christ is so overwhelming and tremendous that we cannot do otherwise than dedicate our bodies to Him as a living sacrifice. If we feel so little inclination to make a total commitment, the reason is that we have not grasped in our hearts the significance of being forgiven our sins.

In the Old Covenant there was the daily burnt offering, in which the sacrificial animal was entirely consumed by flames. Humanly speaking, there was nothing reasonable about this daily slaughtering and burning, for animal blood could not really remove sins. Yet all this had a deep significance. It was foreshadowing Christ's sacrifice at Calvary. Through the mercy which His sacrifice has obtained for us, we should now be moved to offer our very selves; for when the apostle speaks here of the sacrifice of our bodies, he is referring, in fact, to the sacrifice of our whole being. Body and soul are a unity. We are to be completely and utterly surrendered to God. Our dedication should not be half-hearted but as generous as is His overflowing mercy towards us.

Because of our ingrained self-righteousness, we need to ask ourselves again and again whether we do rely on the mercies of God and whether we do respond with total dedication. Are we so aware of the abyss of sin within us that we are overwhelmed with gratitude for His forgiveness? Are we so gripped with the joy of forgiveness that, constrained by the Spirit of God, we dedicate our lives completely to the Lord? Even human happiness can inspire a sacrificial attitude. For instance, during my youth work I used to notice the transformation in girls after they became engaged. Whereas they used to be self-absorbed, now for love of another person they were suddenly willing to put themselves out on his account. How much more does love for Jesus — growing out of repentance and the experience of forgiveness — cause us to forget self and give us the grace to devote ourselves to Him!

This is what Paul means when he says that 'by the mercies of God' we are to offer our very selves as a living sacrifice to Him. Then we will no longer count the missing hours of sleep or the time required for a special effort in our service for Him. Nothing is too much for us. We do not grow annoyed or irritable when an additional task turns up and we think we have no energy left. Moved by the power of His mercy, we demonstrate our love and dedication. If this is not so, our experience of justification by faith is not genuine. We are still held captive by the law, trying to fulfil it because we have to. We have not yet entered the freedom described in Romans 7:1-6.

This total dedication, inspired by the Spirit, must be a living sacrifice. This means it is never static. A lifeless object remains as it is. But a living tree puts out fresh shoots; it bears leaves, blossoms and fruit. It is in a constant state of change. So a living sacrifice is not legalistic. It is flexible. We can't impose hard-and-fast rules, specifying how we will restrict ourselves with regard to sleep, food, personal wishes and interests. That would be a dead sacrifice, because it would again be under the law.

A living sacrifice develops like a living tree. I do not know how and when the leaves and blossoms appear. The Holy Spirit constrains me by the mercies of God and teaches me to fast in one instance but on another occasion to take care of my body (though not pampering it), since otherwise my work will suffer. There will be times when He calls me to give a testimony, even if it costs me much, and other times when He requires me to bring a sacrifice by remaining silent.

It is as the Spirit of *life* that the Holy Spirit will guide me. However, I will respond to His directives only to the extent that I am humbled before Jesus as a wretched but pardoned sinner. The Holy Spirit is gentle. So if He is to effect this total dedication in us, we must be empty and weak in ourselves. And nothing makes us feel so weak in ourselves as being convicted of our sin. But then the Holy Spirit has compassion on us and can use us. He can move us as easily as a gust of wind blows a small soft feather, and we no longer resist and grieve Him by our self-will and inflexibility.

This living sacrifice is to be our 'reasonable service'. Paul was probably thinking of the Temple in Jerusalem, where the worship services took place according to the Old Testament ritual with many animal sacrifices, which humanly speaking were *not* reasonable. They pointed to Jesus' sacrifice. And so, by the mercies of Jesus Christ in the New Covenant, we are called to offer ourselves as our 'reasonable service'. A living sacrifice denotes action, flexibility and spontaneity. A living thing brings forth fruit. A living sacrifice dedicated to God's service is not some pious thought. It is not made in a vacuum. Justification by faith has nothing to do with some dry theory. It is a vital, creative force pulsating through a person's life and resulting in action.

A 'reasonable service' the Lord expects of us especially in our day is that of priestly intercession. If we are to give our bodies as a sacrifice, this also means that we are to pray and plead for our church and nation in a priestly way. This is not to be confused with asceticism. Genuine gratitude for God's mercy will constrain us to give up sleep or certain activities that we enjoy or consider worthwhile, in order to pray for a situation of great need. How much time do we often spend in chatting or reading the newspaper, for instance! How much time we often waste on unnecessary matters. Yet we don't seem to get round to offering a 'reasonable service'. If we were convicted of sin and lived for God, we would. That would be a fruit of our justification by faith.

Our 'whole burnt offering' is also to be holy. From the Old Testament we know that the utensils used in the tabernacle were holy to the Lord (Exodus 30:29). The pans and dishes did not look very different from those the Israelite women used for household purposes. But the ones in the tabernacle were consecrated. They were to be used only for the ceremonial ritual of sacrifice. Similarly, the sacrifice of our bodies is a holy act, transforming our everyday life. In view of the mercies of God, we are to practise this surrender of the body through discipline in eating and drinking, for instance, and by saying *No* to worldly passions (Titus 2:12). By God's grace we have been brought to repentance over the sins of the flesh and have tasted His forgiveness. Should this not compel us to give our bodies as a holy sacrifice?

Here again we are not speaking of law. The devil raises objections at this point. He tries to fool us, saying, 'But if you are justified by faith, then discipline like this is legalism!' But if we have really tasted the forgiveness of Jesus and realize what it has cost Him to atone for our sin, we feel compelled to change our ways. According to Martin Luther, a Christian who is really contrite seeks ways of making amends. And so we are also constrained to make a holy sacrifice of our body in order to help stem the tide of sin and self-indulgence, which is rising everywhere to a frightening extent.

God seeks this holy service from us as members of the Body of Christ. He longs for us to plead and spend ourselves for the redemption of many more souls. Paul writes, for instance: 'I endure everything for the sake of the elect, that they also may obtain the salvation which in Christ Jesus goes with eternal glory' (2 Timothy 2:10) — 'I will most gladly spend and be spent for your souls' (2 Corinthians 12:15). The hunger, thirst and persecution he frequently endured all speak of his total dedication. He was moved by the mercies of God to make this sacrifice of love for the sake of the elect, so that many would be released from their sinful bonds.

May such holy sacrifices be offered among us today with a priestly attitude. The destiny of our nations depends upon it. Jesus became the great High Priest, so that by His suffering and death He might win many priestly souls, who would in turn be capable of offering a 'reasonable service'. When in Christ we are included in this priestly ministry, this in no way implies that we are detracting from Jesus' glory. We can carry out this service only as pardoned sinners, trusting in His mercy. By presenting all our members and faculties as a holy sacrifice, we actually glorify His redemption. Such dedication is a fruit of His redemption.

'Do not be conformed to this world.' This, too, should be a fruit of our justification by faith. We need to ask whether as a result of God's mercy this fruit can be found in us. What is meant by 'this world'? The present age is a period of time under the dominion of the prince of this world. It covers the whole span of human history, beginning with the first Adam, and we are all part of it. By birth and nature we are all children of this world. Nonetheless the challenge rings out: 'Do not be conformed to this world!'

The present age is not yet over, but it is overlapped by a second age, which dawned at Easter with the resurrection of Jesus and which will be consummated at His return. The second age cannot be defined like the first, solely in terms of time. It includes the renewal of our minds. All who belong to the second age, and thus to Christ, ought to know that this epoch must become visible today in that we are transformed by the renewal of our minds.

What does it mean to be not conformed to this world but transformed by the renewal of our minds? Usually, we fail to see the tension between this world and the renewal of our minds. Consequently, we tend to reason as follows: Either I am still of this world, living the old self-centred life and walking in darkness; or else I am in the Kingdom of Jesus Christ and have nothing more to do with this world. But this is not what the apostle Paul means. Though we live *in* this world, we are not to be conformed to it. As children of the new world, we are to break free from this world's domination through an entirely new attitude of mind. Earthly matters, such as eating and drinking, are still part of our lives. We can have happy times together, singing and rejoicing. But now everything is done in relationship to Jesus and in thanksgiving for God's mercy. This is what is new.

The characteristics of this world and its prince are lust for power, greed, covetousness, pleasure-seeking, self-love, a domineering attitude, self-will, and so on. Again, the renewing of our minds means sacrificing ourselves and surrendering body, soul and spirit completely to Jesus. Consequently, our lives will undergo a transformation while we are in this world.

When the mercy of Jesus Christ has gained room in us, we are so captivated by His unmerited love that our attitude to the things of this world changes. We continue to eat and drink, since these are necessities of life, but we do so, as already said, in a priestly spirit. As we go about our daily work, we do so in faith, knowing that only His grace can bless our efforts, and with the longing for Him to be made known and to be glorified in everything we do. We celebrate special occasions, but no longer for our own enjoyment. If our minds are renewed, then our celebrations can only be for the glory of Jesus, bringing Him love and honour. Everything pivots on Him and, as a result, everything is transformed.

So we do not say: *We* must present our bodies as a sacrifice. That would be dismal and forced, and self would be at the centre. Instead what is done in response to the mercy of God always has a glow of happiness about it — quite different from the endeavours of our pious rational self and from self-imposed asceticism. Consequently, the whole of our everyday life is made new through the renewal of our minds. It is said that Fra Angelico, the famous painter of frescoes in Florence, never made a stroke of the brush without prayer. Everything was done in conscious love for Jesus. We, too, have the opportunity of doing everything in prayer, invoking God's blessing. But if instead we follow the pattern of this world as we do our work, it is ultimately self-centred, concerned with *us*, our personal wishes and desires.

When we are transformed people with renewed minds, everything is centred on Jesus: 'What would please *Him*?' 'How can I thank *Him*?' And whenever we find something hard, we do it with the attitude, 'For You, Lord, for You!'

If we really did as the Bible says and refused to let the world squeeze us into its mould, others would be challenged. The effects would also be seen within our church and fellowship. But what we say and do should be motivated by gratitude for God's mercy. Otherwise we will fall into the trap of legalism, becoming Pharisees and hypocrites. The mercy of God is displayed only against the backdrop of His judgment. It is by judgment that light and grace enter the world. Let us pray for the Lord to reveal us *as we are* in His light. When the Lord judges us, we learn to put Jesus at the centre of our lives. Then we are able to discern the will of God and what is good, acceptable and perfect in His sight. Love kindled by the love of Christ is sensitive to His will and to what is honouring to Him, and seeks to do it.

We often complain, 'How can I discern God's will? I just don't know!' This is a sign that we are not under God's mercy. When we are repentant, the Lord becomes more real to us and we are responsive to Him. When we are filled with contrition, we can sense the greatness of His sufferings and become receptive to His will. Love intuitively knows what is going on in the heart of the other person, without being told. It is this same sensitivity which the Lord looks for in us. Often we want to know God's will, just so that we may feel secure, because we do not dare to act in opposition to Him. Such an insurance-policy mentality is sheer egoism. Discernment of God's will should be inspired by love, concern for His honour, and the desire to fulfil His requests.

Knowing God's will comes only through the experience of forgiveness of sin. How many mistakes we make otherwise! If we recognize our need for God's saving grace because of our sins, and if we desire with all our hearts to do His will, then God reveals His will to us. Then we seek His glory. Then we long for Him to be loved and for His wishes to be fulfilled. To such He gives the ability to recognize His will — even in difficult and seemingly meaningless situations. Thus we need only to abandon ourselves to the mercy of God and allow ourselves to be led into the fruit of our justification by faith: the living, holy sacrifice of our bodies, which is our 'reasonable service'. Instead of being conformed to this world, we should allow ourselves to be transformed by God from within by the renewing of our minds. Then, spurred on by love, we will discern what is the good and perfect will of God.

It is vital for all of us to practise this today, in order that we may glorify God in the coming time of testing by our faithfulness and, if He requires it, by the sacrifice of our lives.

Supplementary Reading

by M. Martyria Madauss

JESUS — A PORTRAIT OF LOVE: A Meditation on Matthias Grünewald's Isenheim Altar
64 pages, hard cover, 28 colour plates
This interpretation of the famous paintings with their presentation of the Gospel has been used by God to touch many lives:

While reading the book on a plane, a young American was moved to tears in thanksgiving to Jesus for His sufferings on our behalf. An air hostess, thinking he was distressed, sat down beside him and heard the Gospel as the youth explained the pictures to her. In closing, he added that Jesus had also died for her and was waiting for her to surrender her life to Him. On that flight the air hostess accepted Jesus as her Saviour. Some days later the news carried a report that a plane belonging to the same airline had crashed; and on the list of fatal casualties was the name of that air hostess. A brief encounter was the turning-point of her life, preparing her to meet her Saviour.

In Ethiopia missionaries have used the book as a kind of picture Bible to explain the Gospel to the illiterate.

THE SHIELD OF FAITH 36 pages, handwritten
Short encouraging texts for the daily battle of faith
against sin.

by M. Basilea Schlink

STRONG IN THE TIME OF TESTING 96 pages
As Christians face growing pressures, the need to
prepare for the testing of our faith is even more
urgent than when these texts and prayers were
originally written. We would never be able to bear
the hatred, harassment and persecution in our own
strength. Yet, as Mother Basilea encouragingly
shares, in Jesus Christ we can find all the grace we
need to stand the test of suffering.

REPENTANCE — THE JOY-FILLED LIFE
96 pages
'This book unfolds God's answer to one of the
greatest needs in the churches of our time. If you
are looking for new life, joy and power for your
own spiritual life and for those around you, then
this book is a must.'